REMINISCENCES
OF AN UNLETTERED MAN

Robert Barclay, 1850-1924

REMINISCENCES

OF AN UNLETTERED MAN

ROBERT BARCLAY
1850–1924

FARM SERVANT, TAILOR AND POSTMAN IN
FORGUE AND AUCHTERLESS

edited by
DAVID STEVENSON

ABERDEEN UNIVERSITY PRESS

First published 1985
Aberdeen University Press
A member of the Pergamon Group
© Centre for Scottish Studies, University of Aberdeen 1985

British Library Cataloguing in Publication Data

Barclay, Robert
  Reminiscences of an unlettered man.
  1. Barclay, Robert   2. Scotland — Biography
  I. Title   II. Stevenson, David, *1942-*
  941.1081'092'4   CT828.B3/

ISBN 0 08 032442 8 (flexi)

PRINTED IN GREAT BRITAIN
THE UNIVERSITY PRESS
ABERDEEN

PREFACE

In addition to arranging conferences and seminars the University of Aberdeen Centre for Scottish Studies has, since 1972, undertaken publication of the journal *Northern Scotland* and of pamphlets relating to local history. A further outlet for works relating to northern Scotland has now been provided through co-operation between the Centre and Aberdeen University Press, whereby works edited and prepared for publication by the Centre will be published by AUP in an occasional series. The series begins this year with two contrasting works. *New Light on Medieval Aberdeen* comprises half a dozen short papers seeking to make the results of recent academic research easily accessible to a wide audience, while the *Reminiscences* of Robert Barclay relate the life of a late nineteenth century farm hand, tailor and postman in northern Aberdeenshire.

The *Reminiscences* (as printed by the author in the early 1920s) were brought to the Centre for Scottish Studies in 1984 by Mr Robert W Barclay and Mrs Rosemary Baxter, the former being the author's grandson. Mrs Baxter, a member (and now Secretary) of the Aberdeen and North East Scotland Family History Society, had read the work, and had suggested to Mr Barclay that it might be of some interest to historians. On reading the *Reminiscences* I agreed and, worried by the fact that parts of the printed text (only one copy of which exists) were in danger of deteriorating into complete illegibility, arranged that the Centre should prepare a typed transcript. This difficult task (the text being very blurred and faint in places) was undertaken by Mrs Margaret Croll, with her usual accuracy and efficiency. From this transcript the present edition has been prepared; for once the text was thus available in an easily readable form it became clear that the work merited publication, both as a source for the social historian and as a work which recaptures many aspects of life in the North East a century ago in a way which should appeal to readers in the area and elsewhere. Sadly, though the author was a keen photographer, virtually none of his photographs survive. The work has therefore been illustrated with photographs of street scenes from the George Washington Wilson Collection in Aberdeen University Library. I am most grateful to the Librarian, Mr J M Smethurst, for permission to publish these. The photograph of the author which appears as the frontispiece was supplied by his grandson, though as it was badly damaged it has had to be retouched in places. Robert Walker Barclay has also generously agreed that the unique copy of the *Reminiscences* printed by his grandfather, together with a surviving notebook of his, should be deposited in Aberdeen University Library (in Local Collections and the Department of Manuscripts respectively).

David Stevenson
Director
Centre for Scottish Studies
Aberdeen University

September 1985

INTRODUCTION

Robert Barclay (1850-1924) lived all his life in the parishes of Forgue and Auchterless, which lie to the east of Huntly in north west Aberdeenshire. The son of a handloom weaver who also farmed a croft, Barclay spent his life as a farm servant, a tailor, a shop assistant (briefly) and, finally, as a postman. His life was uneventful in that it contained no great dramas which might have singled him out from his fellows, no involvement in great public issues, no career successfully pursued. He was, in the best sense of the word, an 'ordinary' man, with little to distinguish him from the folk among whom he lived. The only event in his life which could be said to be highly unusual is that he compiled an autobiography, his *Reminiscences*. Moreover Barclay is unusual in his motivation for writing. Those who decide to write the story of their own lives usually believe their lives to be of particular interest, either through their achievements, or through an egotism that insists their experiences must be more significant than that of their fellow men; and of course frequently fame (or notoriety) and egotism are combined. Yet Robert Barclay would have ridiculed the idea that he had any achievements in life to boast of, and his egotism is so limited that he frequently pushes himself into the background of his own autobiography.

Why, then, did Barclay venture to write his *Reminiscences?* The answer appears to be that he became fascinated by the idea of printing a book with his own hands, and that in order to do this he had first to write something to print. He began, it seems, to work on this project after his retirement as a postman in 1921, and at several points in his text the date of writing (or rather of typesetting) is given as 1923-4. But it seems that he had had the ambition of printing a book for many years, for it was inspired by a story he had read in a school book sixty years before concerning William Davy.

Davy's epic achievement in private printing has earned him a place in the *Dictionary of National Biography*. Born in 1743, he became a curate and his *System of Divinity* was published in Exeter (1785-6) in six volumes. Subsequently Davy decided to extend the work to twenty-six volumes, but could not afford to subsidise publication. He therefore constructed a printing press, bought some old type, and from 1795 to 1807 laboriously produced fourteen copies of each of the twenty-six volumes, each running to about 500 pages. Nobody seems to have been much impressed by Davy's theology, but he became so renowned for his perseverance that he was immortalised in moralising school books as an illustration of that virtue. Davy's search for ecclesiastical preferment was even more extended than his printing labours; he at last secured presentation to a vicarage at the age of eighty-three, dying a few months later in 1826.

Davy's story, perhaps a sad one to our eyes but a splendid one to Victorian moralists, clearly impressed the young Robert Barclay, so after retirement he bought a second hand printing press and set to work. His labours were not on Davy's heroic scale, but as he was over seventy when he began work this is hardly surprising. He had only enough type to set one page at a time, and even then he had sometimes to use types of differing sizes, and many minor mistakes remained uncorrected. As he engagingly explains, he found he could easily detect printers' mistakes in books and newspapers, 'but somehow my own escaped my notice, until ... too late for correction'. Many an author will sympathise.

Whatever Barclay's reasons for compiling his *Reminiscences*, is the work worth reprinting? If his life was so quiet and uneventful, lacking the sort of incidents which provide distinctiveness and interest, why should anyone want to read about it? Though it may seem paradoxical at first, the answer is that it is precisely because Barclay's life is so ordinary, so like those of many other folk in the Buchan countryside, that it is so interesting. Most autobiographers are unrepresentative of most of us through their achievements and/or egotism. In the *Reminiscences* we have an account of a working man not very different in his life from thousands of others. Clearly it would be wrong to push this too far; Robert Barclay was an individual, and to claim that he was in all ways typical of his age and station in life would be to deny this individuality that we all possess. Yet reading his account of his life helps us to understand not just what made *him* tick, but what life was like in the countryside of the North East a century ago.

The *Reminiscences* do not form a polished literary work and Barclay describes himself on the title page as 'an unlettered man'. The range of his reading and interests is such that his judgment may be thought too harsh, but such a reaction would probably be to mistake his intention. He is not confessing in shame to being 'an unlettered man'; rather he is making an objective statement about himself. He is pointing out that his formal education had been limited; but in his circumstances there is no shame in this. Indeed, an opposite interpretation is plausible — that he is really rather proud of the fact that though his educational opportunities were limited he has succeeded not only in writing a book but in printing it as well. For this reason it has been decided to call this new edition *Reminiscences of an Unlettered Man*, in place of Barclay's own title *Reminiscences of By-Gone Years*. The latter is disappointingly bland and anonymous, while the new title highlights what is unusual about this particular autobiography, without implying any slight to its author.

Not being a carefully structured literary work, the *Reminiscences* tend at times to meander from one topic to another in a rather inconsequential way — as spoken reminiscences do. This in some ways helps bring us closer to Barclay, giving the air of listening to an old man talking of his distant youth but occasionally digressing. Though the work is built on a narration of Barclay's life, he does to some extent keep the reader at a distance from his emotions. For example he cannot — or will not — describe the death of his wife and what such an event meant to him. Mentioning his wife's death in the context of needing to find a housekeeper might seem almost callous, but it is rather that such moments are private, and not to be shared. To analyse his emotions in his own words is either impossible for him, or is avoided as too revealing; instead he falls back on sentimental descriptions of the impact of such events culled from popular literature.

The *Reminiscences* are mainly concerned with anecdotes concerning himself and his friends, at school and at work. Wider issues only encroach insofar as they are responsible for the disappearance of the world of his younger days. Crofts are swallowed up to extend existing farms, or are amalgamated to form new farms; rural trades, such as his father's hand-loom weaving and his own tailoring, collapse. As a result of such changes, touns or hamlets such as the one he grew up in are disappearing. Rural unemployment and consequent depopulation have destroyed a way of life. His own abandonment of tailoring reflects the decline of the trade (though he does not explicitly say so); and, inadvertently, he contributes to this decline by becoming a postman, for the parcel post makes possible the cheap distribution throughout the countryside of mass-produced clothes and other goods.

That the rural life that Barclay describes had partly vanished by the time he wrote was of course a matter of sadness to him; but it makes his account all the more interesting today. Most of the events and anecdotes he recounts may be petty in themselves; but they are significant for the glimpses they give us of a 'world we have lost' — of what it was like to attend a country school over a century ago, to be a tailor's apprentice, to work as a cattle-man and try to discover the secrets of the Horseman's Word from which you were excluded. Work had a dominant part to play in determining the pattern of Barclay's life, but play and socialising were also important — and combine with work as young tailors play tricks on each other and talk and joke with friends who drop in to keep them company as they work at night. Total Abstinence claimed Barclay's allegiance, and linked up with his interest in workers' mutual improvement classes. Reading widened his outlook by giving him an interest in natural history and local antiquities. Wider horizons in a more literal sense were represented by visits to Banff (to learn photography), Aberdeen and Shetland; unfortunately he tells us nothing about his activities as a photographer, though the fact that he possessed a tripod camera at the time of his death suggests that he had a continuing interest in that hobby. Another aspect of his interest in how things work is, of course, indicated by his printing of the *Reminiscences*. His home may have lain deep in the countryside, but it was by no means isolated. Nor is it a static life; the well-known movement of farm servants from farm to farm in the countryside was, if Barclay is typical, shared by apprentices and journeymen in the tailoring trade.

Recent publications on the history of the Scottish countryside have, not surprisingly, concentrated on agriculture and its workforce, but a recent essay by Gavin Sprott is particularly helpful in understanding the lives of tradesmen such as Robert Barclay — 'The country tradesman', in *Farm Servants and Labour in Lowland Scotland, 1770-1914* edited by T M Devine (Edinburgh, 1984).

In compiling the *Reminiscences* Robert Barclay evidently relied on a number of notebooks in which he had recorded miscellaneous information. One of these has survived, containing lists of numbers of letters and parcels he delivered each week for the twenty-seven years he was a postman (the totals are given in the *Reminiscences*); copies of newspaper classified advertisements, death notices and obituaries,

1906-12 (evidently often composed by him and inserted in the papers for others — and occasionally for himself); notes, mainly on castles, copied from guide books and histories; a few extracts from Robert Hall's diary (mentioned below); and lists of postal orders, 1912-21.

Barclay evidently printed only two copies of his work, and only one survived, with the following title page:

REMINISCENCES OF BY-GONE YEARS

BY

ROBERT BARCLAY

"Reader. I hope you be so kind
With oversights that here you'll find
To pass them by as best you can
For I am an unlettered man".

AUCHTERLESS:

Printed & Published by the Author

Unfortunately the poor quality paper, pink in colour, that he used is decaying rapidly, and the ink has often spread to such an extent that the blurred printing verges on illegibility.

In preparing this new edition of the *Reminscences* a limited amount of editorial work has been undertaken to make the work more easily accessible to readers. Occasional spelling and other errors, reflecting Barclay's difficulties in printing rather than ignorance, have been silently corrected, and abbreviations have been extended. Attempts have been made to bring his erratic punctuation into line with his meaning: how many authors have the candour to admit that 'Punctuation was guess work, not having studied that branch of learning'? Some cuts have been made, shortening the text by about twenty per cent. The complete text runs to about 52,000 words; Barclay admits that this is almost twice as long as he had intended, and some sections can be omitted without significantly reducing its value. His two papers delivered to a mutual improvement class, on a Trip to Shetland and on Total Abstinence, have been drastically pruned, leaving only enough to provide samples of such works, and some of his long quotations from other writers have been omitted or shortened. An exception, however, has been made in the case of his extracts from the manuscript diary of Robert Hall, a farmer who died in 1833; these, and an account of Hall's life, form a memoir within a memoir that deserves printing in full. Finally, a few passages in which Barclay digresses into matters irrelevant to the topic he is dealing with, or into anecdotes which seem totally pointless, have been omitted. In all such cases the point at which omissions occur have been marked in the text. Occasional additions have been made in square brackets, adding a word where this is necessary to the sense of a passage, providing the meaning of an obsolete word, or indicating the contents of a passage which has been omitted. The outline family tree has been prepared from information contained in the *Reminiscences*, supplemented by the details the author included in a 'Family Register' inserted at the beginning of his copy of Thomas Haweis, *The Evangelical Expositor; or, A Commentary on the New Testament* (Glasgow, 1841).

Days of my youth, the long pass'd years
    of childhood round me rise:
I see them glistening through the tears
    that start into my eyes.
The joys that round my bosom press'd,
    when thoughtless, young, and wild
Come like a sunbeam o'er my breast:
    again I am a child.

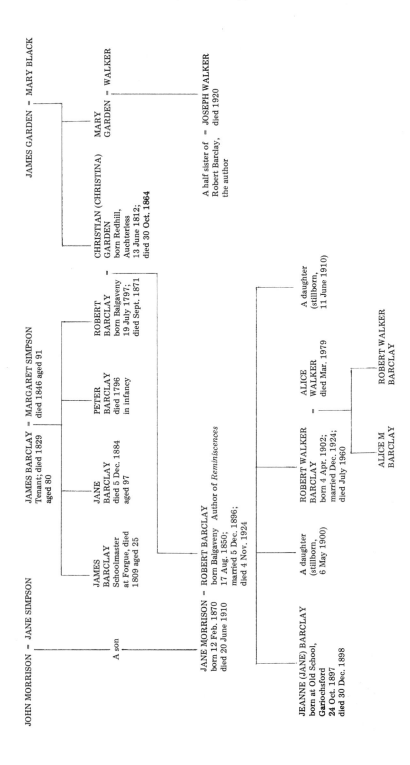

JAMES GARDEN = MARY BLACK

JOHN MORRISON = JANE SIMPSON

JAMES BARCLAY = MARGARET SIMPSON
Tenant; died 1829   died 1846 aged 91
aged 80

MARY
GARDEN = WALKER

CHRISTIAN (CHRISTINA)
GARDEN
born Redhill,
Auchterless
13 June 1812;
died 30 Oct. 1864

A half sister of = JOSEPH WALKER
Robert Barclay,   died 1920
the author

A son

JAMES
BARCLAY
Schoolmaster
at Forgue, died
1809 aged 25

JANE
BARCLAY
died 5 Dec. 1884
aged 97

PETER
BARCLAY
died 1796
in infancy

ROBERT
BARCLAY
born Balgaveny
19 July 1797;
died Sept. 1871

=

JANE MORRISON = ROBERT BARCLAY   Author of *Reminiscences*
born 12 Feb. 1870   born Balgaveny
died 20 June 1910   17 Aug. 1850;
                      married 5 Dec. 1896;
                      died 4 Nov. 1924

A daughter
(stillborn,
6 May 1900)

ROBERT WALKER
BARCLAY
born 4 Apr. 1902;
married Dec. 1924;
died July 1960

=

ALICE
WALKER
died Mar. 1979

A daughter
(stillborn,
11 June 1910)

JEANNE (JANE) BARCLAY
born at Old School,
Gariochsford
24 Oct. 1897
died 30 Dec. 1898

ALICE M
BARCLAY

ROBERT WALKER
BARCLAY

REMINISCENCES OF BY-GONE YEARS

"There comes a voice that awakes my Soul: it
is the voice of years that are gone; they roll
before me with all their deeds". — Ossian

I was born at Knowes, Balgaveny, Forgue, Aberdeenshire,
on Saturday 17 August 1850. Knowes has no attractive surroundings, being shut in from the outside world by low hills
on all sides but for an outlet on the east, through which the
turnpike to Aberdeen via Inverurie runs, and alongside of
which is a small burn fed by local springs, which joins the
Ythan at Knockleith, Auchterless 3 miles eastward; having
ere then been joined by other two on the left bank, rising at
Upper Lenshie and Old Yoach; also one on the right bank,
rising at Upperthird.

The view from Knowes eastward includes part of Auchterless and Fyvie, also part of the country east of Fyvie. The
view, commencing at the turnpike includes the brae of Hassiewells on Hatton estate; [it] has 5 farms, the lower ones good,
the upper just middling. The brae terminates in a hill, about
800 ft. above sea level, locally called the Kirkhill. West is the
Brownhill, once adorned with a wood, but now cultivated.
On the north is Balgaveny wood; on the east Brae of Largue,
Denmoss, and Gariochsford, terminating at the meal mill,
now a ruin, a mile below my birthplace.

At the time of my birth and for 20 years following, the
Knowes had 4 crofts, one occupied by a blacksmith, another,
a larger, by John Skinner, who owned a horse named "Jacky".
John died, and his relatives kept the holding for several years
when they went to America, and were succeeded by William
Loban who held it until old age compelled him to retire;
then it was added to the one previously tenanted by Robert
Fraser (our next door neighbour), whose relatives now hold
it. My father's croft, a 5 acre one, was added to Robert
Fraser's in 1864; my mother dying in October that year.
We were, however, allowed to remain in the house till after
my father's death in 1871. Thus three small holdings became
1 farm; and another nearby was added to a neighbouring one.
This still goes on. Lairds and factors are blamed; but they
lack no help when required. I give an instance of it. An old

widow finding it necessary to leave her croft, told a friend so. An adjoining farmer hearing, offered to drive her to the factor's house 7 miles away to let her resign; an offer willingly accepted. The widow saw the factor and resigned; the farmer saw him too, with the result that at the term the croft became part of his farm.

The houses at Knowes were all thatched, and had three apartments, a but, a closet, and a ben or kitchen with a hanging lum. The closet had no fire-place, and served as a bedroom and milkhouse. My father's house differed from the others internally, the room being used as a shop. To make up for it, a room was added to the kitchen and entered therefrom; in this room I first saw the light. Of that event I have no recollection. At the time of my birth as stated our room was a shop. It was a grocer's one for two years after my birth, subsequently a hand-loom weaver's workshop, and my earliest recollection is of seeing my father following that calling, he having learned from his father, who carried on weaving at Knowes when Forgue had about 100 weavers in it. I remember when there were but three, the last being the late James Scott, Bogs of Raich. My great-grandfather, a tailor, lived at Knowes so my grandfather may have been born there. The following is on a gravestone in Auchterless graveyard —

> "In memory of the late James Barclay tenant in Bilgaveny Parish of Forgue. He died 8th Sept. 1828 aged 80 years. His Spouse Margaret Simpson died 10th Jan. 1846 aged 91 years. Their son Peter died in infancy in 1796. Their son James Barclay A.M. late schoolmaster at Forgue died 1st May 1809 aged 25 years".

Although unrecorded on the stone, my father, mother, two aunts, and other relatives are interred near it; the last of the family Jane Barclay, (my aunt) died at Glenythan 5th December 1884 aged 97 years, and is interred at Ythanwells, in grave no. 2, G Section. It will be seen that on the father side I come of a comparatively long lived race. Not so on the mother side; although one or two uncles passed the alloted span.

PARENTAGE

My father was born at Knowes July 1797, and died there September 1871; and practically spent all his days in his native parish. The little schooling he got was at Forgue 4 to 5 miles distant. That was when his brother was teaching there. I have heard that my uncle pursued his studies in the dark evenings lying on his back before the fire, its light illuminating the book. He was studying for the ministry, but death changed his plans. "Such is life".

My mother (whose name was Christian Garden) was born at Redhill, Auchterless, June 1812. The family consisted of 6 sons and 3 daughters. Their father was a labouring man, named James Garden; his wife's name was Mary Black. James was droll and many stories were told of him. He was a bit of an astronomer, and was afraid of thunder. When thunder clouds appeared, he made tracks for home as fast as possible, went to bed, while it was said that his wife rang the girdle during the thunder-peals to drown the noise. My mother had a twin sister named Mary, who died at Arnbead, Auchterless, about 1854. Her son Joseph Walker who died July 1920; was married to my half-sister; being thus brother-in-law as well as cousin. My grandmother made whisky, quite common in those days. My mother told me how it was made and the narrow escapes they often had of being caught by the gauger; but owing to the good-feeling among people in those days, the exciseman had ill getting hold of defaulters, as few would give any information against their neighbours, but warned each other when they knew the officer was coming; so his visit usually was fruitless, although at times some were caught. Once my grandfather's house was searched, but nothing illicit was found. Every place was searched but the cradle; in which a child lay asleep, with a "pig" of whisky at its feet. The brewing utensils were hid in peat-stacks, the lint steep, or under the house floor; the malt was often kept a long way from the house. While rambling in Drumsennie wood, far from any house, my mother came on a store of malt among whins; on going home she told her mother who knew about it. My mother's school days were limited to a few months at James Beattie's a souter in Gordonstone; [and at] J. Pounds, the cobbler. My mother's early days were hard, often going barefooted in winter, warming her feet among the hot ashes in the ash pit, moss fuel being abundant then but scarce now. I sat in the long evenings and heard many a tale of by-gone days: the following

Alarming Incident

happened at Knowes where she was fee'd. The man she kept
house for died and, as was customary the neighbours came to
dress and lay out the corpse. This was duly gone about, the
dead man being put into the room. The living were in the kitchen, when all on a sudden a loud noise was heard where the
dead lay, a rush was made for the door by all, except my
mother, who knew what had happened; and a lame woman,
unable to join in the stampede. Someone fell behind the door,
preventing its being opened, so ere anyone got out, matters
were explained; the cause of alarm was the bursting of a pig
of ale in the room press. I may mention that it was night
when this occurred.

> "Childhoods' years now pass before me,
> Forms and scenes of long ago".

My father's early days were spent under better conditions
than my mother's, yet his schooldays too were short. I have
said that my earliest recollection of him was as a hand-loom
weaver, and in early life I assisted him in that capacity, which
consisted in handing him the warp thread by thread as he put
them through the "heedels"; a rather tedious job for a young
chap. I also turned round a roller called the "beam" on which
the warp was wound. The warp was got from messrs. Spence,
Huntly, 11 miles distant and thither I tramped now and then
for it. My father played the bagpipes, a half sized set supplied
with wind from a bellows worked by an arm. Refering to a
bagpipe tutor I find that the scale extends from G on the 2nd
line of the stave to high A on the 1st added or "ledger line",
above the stave, giving 9 notes, viz. G, A, B, C, D, E, F, G, &
A, which are produced by opening and closing certain holes
in the chanter. My father by what he called "pinching", extended the range a few notes, by half-opening the back hole
with his thumb nail; but I do not know what holes in addition
to this were opened or closed to give the extension. I have
seen this device mentioned in a newspaper, in answering a
query on pipe music. My father frequently played at marriages,
raffles, Old Yule gatherings etc. When the late King Edward
(then Prince of Wales) was married, he was piper to the
scholars attending the school at Gariochsford, who were

marched to a social meeting convened near the Free Church, Forgue, in honour of the royal wedding, in March 1863. Years previous, he played them in peculiar circumstances: I got a burn and ere it could be dressed I required a "spring" on the pipes, a request granted, and so under the soothing strains of pipe-music my burn was dressed. Frequently, the young folks near us came to our house for a fireside dance, but I never learned how to go through the reel. An elderly woman, Meggie Guthrie came and took part, it gave us great fun to see her dancing; she stuck her hands into her sides, leaped high, both feet up together, and thus through the reel she went, causing the utmost delight and amusement to all. I knew most of the tunes, usually naming the one to play, and whether quick or slow we danced to them. Some of the tunes I still remember, among others, "Miss Forbes' Farewell to Banff. The Quaker's Wife. Lochaber No More" with its slow mournfull, appealing strains; and many more, including, "The White Cockade, The Highland Laddie, Lord Lennox' March, O'er the Hills and far away; Kenmure's on and awa", and many others grave and gay, too numerous to mention.

My mother's favourite tune was entitled 'He's coming here', etc; and words, of which the following are two lines, were sung to it; "He's coming here, and he will be here. He's coming here for a' that. He's coming bonnie o'er the hills. That will take me fae ye a' yet, etc." Another tune, OLD ADAM, had words that were sung to it, but are now forgotten. "We never miss the water, till the well runs dry". I remember my father relating that once, when on a visit to Macduff, a few friends went out in a boat, for a pleasure sail; he had the pipes with him. When out at sea, they came across a ship, the "JACKEY TAR", the captain took them aboard; where they were well treated, while he discoursed his music. After spending a pleasant hour or two they were put into their boat. They were taken up on one side of the ship, and put off on the other. This was looked on as a mark of respect.

HIGHLAND PETER

I must not forget one who occasionally joined in our social mirth; an old man, PETER STUART, a pedlar, from

Huntly, who paid us visits when on his rounds. He came in the afternoon staying till next morning. He was a highland-man, hence the name of 'Highland Peter'. I was pleased to see him, as his visit meant a penny for me, a big sum in those days. Peter joined in the dance, sang songs, mostly Gaelic, and told stories, with a touch of the supernatural in them; his stock of goods varied; sometimes draperies, then rennet ("yirnen"), and ancn [?] wooden caps [bowls] and laddles. But the passing years told on both pack and person. Once he came with caps and laddles, and I, next day accompanied him on the way to Fyvie. The roads were in a very slippery state. Peter had a custom of taking short runs every now and again, when walking on the road. We had reached Lower Thorniebank safely, when off he set on one of them, at the same time saying to me, "Come on Rob, come on Rob". Scarce had he done with speaking when out beneath him went his feet and down he fell on his back, his caps and laddles under him. The poor man spoke of the risk we ran of breaking our bones by such falls, but scarcely could I refrain from laughing at his fall. Having got up and again shouldered his birn [burden], we went on our way, and no further mishap befell us. Peter visited us for many years but the time came that we saw him no more. He spoke nicely of my mother, calling her "kind and couthie". Few now remain of those who joined in the social mirth of those days.

CHARACTERS

There were many of the wandering class who visited our district. One was John Milne, a poet, from Glenlivet. He wrote as follows, "Johnnie Milne of Livet's Glen, Who wrote it down with his own pen, Came all the way to Turra toon. To show the world's turned upside doon. The farmers, lairds, and clergy here, Screw down men's wages every year, We'll leave themselves to plough and saw, And go to the lands of America". Another was John Adams, known as Kilbaddie, as he came from a place so named in Grange. I am not sure if the following lines are by him or by some other would-be poet. "Come hearken my friends, I will sing you a song. Of parts of the country where you do belong; There's Banffshire, and Moray, good friends I have seen. But now I must mention the Shire Aberdeen. There's Boynsmill, and Placemill, Auchaber, Drumblair; These I'll no pass by, though I mention nae mair. In Auchterless the houses are braw, Such superfine farmers I scarce ever saw. Long may they live; and prosperous be, This goodhearted people are a' kind to me. The parish Kingedward I scarce can pass by, When I go down to Buchan it lies in my way". Here my memory fails. One who sold small wares was called "Bundles". Another was knows as "Yirnins" as he sold that commodity [rennet]. Then a respectable old man, John Murray, sold books and finally tea. Another respectable character was David Dougal, a silk handloom weaver who lost work by the introduction of powerlooms. I must not forget simple Willie Valentine, whose stock of goods latterly was so small that he was allowed to move about without a pedlar's certificate. Someone remarked to him, they heard he was dead, Willie admitted having heard it too, but said, "he kent it wis a lee as seen's he h'ard it". I knew of this, and said the same to him, but the reply I got was, "Yes, and burried in a copper coffin". There was Michael Aitken from Aberdeen, with one leg, a broken-down schoolmaster. Another, from Glenbucket, once held a post in Elgin Academy, and latterly taught in Fyvie. Sandy Chisholm, a drover, was born in Urry parish, and drowned in the Urie, Aberdeenshire. William Schofield, another drover, was a noted salmon poacher; from him I got a tip on baiting hooks to take trout. Many others of both sexes I can recollect but pass them by.

Two brothers, Irishmen, rag collectors, Walter and James Welsh, from Aberdeen, put up with our neighbour Robert Fraser. He and his wife, Bell Harper, were kind to the wandering class, in helping them and giving them a night's quarters. Once a tramp in want of a night's shelter, was put into the barn by Mr Fraser, who forgot to mention this on retiring to the house. He remembered afterward he had left a bag in the barn that he should have brought in. It was dark, but, knowing where to find it, two members of the household went to fetch it, taking no light with them. They groped their way to where the bag lay, when the man amongst the straw coughed, causing them to go out much faster than they entered; and without waiting to ask who was there, made for the house as fast as possible, trying who would get in first.

ROBERT GORDON: ASTRONOMER

Perhaps the most interesting of all the many characters who visited the district was the above, better known as "Stronnie", as he professed to have some knowledge of the movements of the heavenly bodies. He was a painter to trade, but had taken to a wandering life, he liked a dram, and it was difficult at times to get rid of him unless he got one. When I was quite young he came round and, Mrs Fraser wishing to be clear of him, went into the room, instructing her oldest girl not to say where she was. I was there, but got no instructions to be silent. In came Stronnie, with a lum hat, a good deal battered, on his head, and a cane in his hand. He asked the girl where her mother was, but as her answer was unsatisfactory, he made to go away; when I informed him she was in the room, and so she soon appeared. When I was serving my time as a tailor at Mr Webster's, Balgaveny, in after years, the following occured. In addition to grocery, tailoring, etc., there was a drug shop; James T. Shepherd being druggist, and one who enjoyed a joke; and played tricks on unsuspecting callers. He put a shovel on the fire that had certain chemicals on it, that exploded with a sharp report, alarming the holder of the shovel, who suspected nothing of that to occur. Our workshop was above the drug one, and, it was nothing unusual to hear a loud report, a scream, and the noise of a shovel falling on the floor all following in quick succession, as some unsuspecting mortal had been initiated into the mystery of the Shovel. Another thing was to get people to hold the handles of a magnete electric machine, (supposed to be a clock), while it was being wound up. This was done and the wires kept in contact till the speed was well up, then they were separated which made the holder cry out, being unable to let the handles go. I forget if Stronnie ever was trapped by the above, but once when visiting the place, a proposal was made to bring his Satanic majesty upon him, and this was to be accomplished by burning spirits of wine on salt which, done in the dark, gives all a ghastly and death-like appearance. As preparations were being carried out, Stronnie was subjected to a deal of horse-play, this he resented, and seizing a four-legged stool he made more than one look for safety. The foreman tailor failed to get out of the way in time, and got a blow on his leg. Stronnie left, and went to North Gariochsford, seeking shelter in a cart hung by the backchain in the cart shed, but he had not been there long when the hook gave way, and down fell the cart with poor Stronnie therein. A short time before he met his death by drowing in the Ythan at Reamshill, Fyvie, he came into our workshop one dark night, wet and bespattered with mud. He was at Mains of Hassiewells, and in coming from that place, fell into a ditch on the roadside, conveying water to the mill-dam. He attributed it to the influence of the planet Venus; adding, that he would get a better duck yet; which proved but too true in a short time. He may have had some presentiment as to how life's journey would end, I cannot tell, but I was an ear-witness to the above remark. The following is on a stone over his grave in Fyvie graveyard.

> "Sacred to the Memory of ROBERT GORDON known as the 'ASTRONOMER', who perished in the YTHAN near REAM-HILL, on the 21st JANUARY 1867. His body was discovered on the 3rd MARCH following and interred here. Cheerful, contented harmless and honest, homeless and unknown to relatives He wandered over this district for upwards of a quarter of a century. To mark his last resting place, the Public have erected this Memorial,
>> This is mine my lowly lot,
>> Here I lie and envy not;
>> Peer or peasant read who may,
>> Remember there's a dying DAY".

A FORTUNE AND A MISFORTUNE

What I am now about to narrate happened long, long ago. I have no date. A postal packet came from abroad, addressed to some of my forbears, for which a sum, too big for them to pay, was charged. A relative was allowed to pay for, and keep the packet. It had been of considerable value, and some notice about it appeared in an Aberdeen newspaper, which led to someone going on horseback through the district, to buy up copies of the paper so as to suppress if possible the windfall, and in doing this, a young animal was "ridden to death". It was after receipt of this packet that a bone-mill was started at Knockleith, abolished long ago. It stood on the left bank of the Ythan, above the mansion-house stables. If the packet had a fortune in it, it was a misfortune to my forefathers that they were too poor to pay for it. How things are all changed today; for a small sum packets large or small go to or come from the ends of the earth.

In my father's youth there lived in Balgaveny an old man who saw soldiers passing through the district on their way to Culloden. I have a razor that belonged to an old pensioner named Macleod, who lived in Balgaveny, and who was wounded at the siege of Badajoz in Spain, stormed by the British under Wellington in 1812. The following certificate of character I reproduce:

> "I have been acquainted with the bearer, ROBERT BAR-CLAY, my Tenant in Bilgaveny, Parish of Forgue, from his infancy, and can recommend him as a very sober, honest, and industrious young man, being always punctual in his engagements and very trust worthy".

(Signed)
And. Jamieson

Cushnie
12 March, 1830

A NARROW ESCAPE

It was previous to my school days that I narrowly escaped death from drowning. Our well was at the edge of a bog, on the burnside, at the lower end of my father's croft. In it there was a trout at which I often had a look. A drain flowed into the well and in order to see up it I had to lie down on a sloping bank and gaze up the drain. In so doing I unfortunately slipped into the well, and would have perished, but for the timely arrival of my mother, who was working in the vicinity. About this period of my life I had another water experience, but of a less alarming nature. I now and then needed a drink during the night, and to be handy a jug with water was put on a shelf above our heads, one night I asked for a drink, but, the jug's contents was knocked down on my face causing me to "gluff" and cry that I was chocked. I need hardly say that night-drinks were seldom needed after this. Another water incident once brought me punishment when I scarcely deserved it. I was amusing myself at the outlet of a drain, where the noise of the rushing water made me deaf to sound farther afield. My mother had, unknown to me, been calling to me to come home but I heeded not. All on a sudden I was seized and punished for disregarding calls I never heard. Such does occur at times.

SCHOOLDAYS

" 'Tis a mournful story, Thus in the ear of pensive eve to tell, Of morning's firm resolve the vanished glory, Love's honey left ungathered in the bell, And flowers of mercy dead, that might have bloomed so well". So wrote some poet and how true his words are of many a life if reviewed, and by-gone years remembered that cannot be recalled, nor lived over again and redeemed.

The first three years of my schooldays were spent at a woman's school, at Mains of Hassiewells, a good half-mile from our house. Like most houses in the district, it was a low thatched one, the kitchen end serving as school-room. Many years afterwards it was a cottar house, and finally a store for farm implements. Now nothing remains to mark its site. The mistress MARGARET AULD, usually called "MEGGIE", was lame and used crutches, one being sufficient indoors. Meggie was a rather illnatured body and among her pupils had favourites, I being one of them. I do not think I ever was punished with her strap, which she could use with effect — although, I have at times seen it taken out, and punishment threatened. I was one of those who occasionally carried to her a flagon of milk, or a "print" of butter, which was supposed to help win her friendship. I do not know when she began teaching: I went to her school in 1856, and many had finished their schooldays ere then. Ten years later she had a few scholars, but they dwindled away, and about 1867, she left the district, ultimately dying (I think) in New Maud Poorhouse. Meggie lacked the qualifications for putting her pupils very far on in learning: reading, writing, committing to memory, and a little plain sewing for the girls, brought her to "the end of her tether". Arithmetic, grammar, and geography were unknown. I have mentioned her ability to use the strap with effect; there was another form of punishment that the girls came

under when their sewing displeased her, viz., bringing her
finger, with the thimble on it, into sudden contact with their
brows. Yet with all her faults, she did good, and served her
day and generation well. I have already stated my disapproval
of abolishing of crofts and small holdings. Our way to school
was past a croft, long ago added to an adjoining farm. It was
occupied by a widow who on leaving it went to one a few
miles away, which at her death, was added to a larger one;
and still matters move in the same old rut. How I long to see
it abolished. But to return. Once after passing this widow's
house, on my way to school, I turned [back], she tried to
catch me but I got off. My mother met and punishing me,
sent me to school and I never turned again while at this school.

HOUSE BREAKING

It was in the year 1856, or '57 that my father's house was
broken into, and several articles and money stolen. The thieves
belonged to the wandering class — Kelly by name. More
money was expected but they were disappointed. My father
went to St Sair's Fair, near Colpy, with a cow for sale, and on
his way thereto saw the Kellies, also going to the Fair. Being
acquainted with my father, they asked if the cow was for sale,
and being told so had likely resolved to get the price, as their
visit was just after the market. Fortunately the cow was not
sold, and so their booty in money was under £1. The first to
see the thieves (a man and a woman), was our neighbour,
John Skinner, who was early astir, and had his suspicions
aroused by their movements; they passed Hassiewells in the
direction of Netherthird. My father upon getting out of bed
found his clothes amissing from a chair where he put them on
going to bed; they were found in the workshop, and now it
was seen that entrance had been made at a window. Neighbours were informed, and I awoke to see them moving about,
looking into presses, drawers, etc. that had been disturbed.
There was no constable at Forgue at that time, so the one,
named Dow, at Auchterless was applied to, who found the
Kellies in a cote at Badenscoth. Several articles belonging to
us were found with them, including towels, with my mother's
initials on them; some sweets, wrapped in a paper, on which I
had scribbled — I had not begun to write — and which was in

the window by which entrance was made. Meal was taken from a barrel and a long black hair was left in it; the woman's hair was black. Coin corresponding with that amissing, was also on them, but, as my father could not prove it as his, they were allowed to keep it. So they lost not all the fruits of their night visit. Everything my father identified as belonging to us, he was allowed to take — money excepted. The Fiscal paid us a visit over it but, somehow I think it ended there, and they got off: it was but for a time, however, for in a short time some of them got into trouble, and into jail. After this they did not again appear in our district. It was a mystery how they got in and moved about without being heard as they carried out their work in a way that would have done credit to professional house breakers.

My next move was to the Free Church school at Gariochs-ford erected after 1843, when the late John Mathieson was minister at Forgue. Mr Ritchie was teacher, but owing to ill health resigned, and soon after died. I was only two weeks under him. He was succeeded by John Pyper, who stayed a few years, and was followed by others, who stayed, some, for long and some for short periods; until the introduction of the Education Act, after which a school, in keeping with its requirements was built at Largue, and Gariochsford school, though still retaining the name, was turned into a dwelling house.

I lost sight of Mr Pyper for many years. Subsequently he turned up as a book canvasser; and died in Aberdeen in comparatively poor circumstances.

I put me down as a favourite with Meggie Auld, but did not regard myself as being one of Mr Pyper's; at least I came in for a fair amount of punishment. I expect it was required. I nearly always failed in the Shorter Catechism lesson, the hearing of which was confined to a certain day of the week. Many and varied were the devices I had recourse to, in order to escape going to school on that particular day, but alas for me, they often failed. At times I feigned sickness but, after the school was in I speedily recovered. Again I would lose sight of my catechism, and would not go to school without one; another was got, but I would return in a great plight, after being nearly at school, having discovered that the leaf required that day was amissing. By this time the school is in and so this device gave me one day's respite, but could scarcely be repeated. So a new way of escape had to be tried,

next week. I left for school at a certain time so I put the
hands of the clock back, in order to make me late, and so
have a good reason for turning (it was my intention to put it
right unobserved), but the old "wag-at-the-wa' ", struck unexpectedly when I was tampering with it, giving me such a
fright that I never meddled with it again. I give one instance
to show how small a mistake led to punishment. One day the
answer to question 90 fell to me, which is as follows:— "That
the word may become effectual to salvation, we must attend
thereunto with diligence, preparation, and prayer, receive it
with faith and love, lay it upon our hearts, and practise it in
our lives". All went well till I came to the word practise: unfortunately I said restore. "You restore", said the teacher,
"I'll give you something to restore you a little", at the same
time producing the strap from his desk, and so I got punished
for one mistake. There was one lesson, however, that was
impressed upon my memory while at this school and which
has proved beneficial to me ever since. At this stage of life
I had imbibed slight pilfering propensities. The master took
from the scholars anything he saw them working with during
school hours, that might have a tendency to draw their attention from their lessons, so whatever it was from a marble to a
knife had to be given up and was kept in the desk until the
harvest vacation when it was given back to the owner. One
day, unobserved, I took from the desk, which had no lock, a
knife belonging to a boy James Deuchars. It was soon missed,
and the master was informed that I had one like it. I showed
him the knife, but cleared myself as I thought by saying that
it had been bought at the shop at Badenscoth. (I had been
seen with it at home, but said I found it, and so was allowed
to retain it meantime). The master said he would see my
father at night, and hear what he had to say about it; sure
enough, he kept his word. I was very uneasy all the rest of
the day, and went to bed earlier than usual, hoping the master
would forget to come. I had not, however, been long in bed,
when a knock came at the door, and on its being opened who
should enter but the schoolmaster. My parents were pleased
to see him; my mother, addressing me, said "O laddie gin
ye'd kent 'at the maister had been comin' ye widna beddet".
So fine did I ken, and ill did I relish the visit. The talk went
on for a time upon general topics, and when these were well
talked over, my father changed the subject by asking how I
was getting on at school. He replied that it was a case about
me that had brought him over, and so the tale of the knife

was soon told. I had no subterfuge now, and got off easier than I expected to do, and certainly than what I deserved. I was daily cautioned, before leaving for school; as also questioned on my return home, as to my behaviour, but I never again committed a like offence. The lessons taught by the stolen knife, had a beneficial and lasting effect. The boy got his knife without waiting till harvest. He and I were always friendly, and I am glad to say that this incident did not mar our friendship. I was called a thief for a short time, but by and by it was forgotten.

I got into trouble at this school over our arithmetic book, it being minus the answers, which were in a "key", and to which we did not have access. We worked our sums on our slates, putting the result on the back of them. Next day, one of the elder boys went round with the "key" to see if we had our sums correctly done. If we were on favourable terms with these lads, they sometimes said we were right when we were wrong; sometimes, we could get an answer or two in advance, by paying a trifle for them. By this, or similar methods I had got to the end of my book, and approached the master with a desire to get one further advanced; he seemed surprised at my progress, and selecting a few questions from my finished (?) book, sent me to my seat to work them out, promising me a handsome sum if I did them correctly. Here I was fairly cornered. I could not do them. I did not even try, but kept looking at, and laughing at those near me to help to keep me from crying. The master meantime remarking, that he would soon make me laugh in another fashion; and sure enough it was so. Another incident, which in no way reflects credit to my character happened at this school and should have preceded the knife one. Most of the books belonged to the school and were often in a rather dilapidated condition, having passed through several hands. (A soiree was held occasionally, to raise funds for their upkeep). One day, a leaf was amissing in my book, and dreading the consequences, I, unknown to another boy took a leaf from his one and put it into mine. When his turn to read came he was silent, as he could not find the place; but his silence soon broke, for the poor lad got punished, when it should have been me. I was sorry for him, yet all the same I failed to step forward and tell the truth, and take the punishment. I was a wee bit tricky both in and out of school; but, despite a fair amount of precaution, I was nearly always found out, as the following incident will show. On a roadside near our house were whin bushes. I got hold of matches one evening, and setting fire to one of them was into the house again in a minute or two, as if nothing had happened, supposing that no one had seen me, and that I would not be suspected. Whether this was so I cannot say, but, a few days later, I met John Shearer, who lived at the school house (his wife was housekeeper to Mr Pyper). The day was wet, and John said so to me, to this I assented, he then said, "The whins winna burn very we'l the day". I took guilt upon me and went away, found out! It was at this school that I got my first lessons in vocal music. We were taught by a Mr Cleriehew from Aberdeen, who taught us in school hours, and had classes for adults at night. In addition to lessons from the modulator, we learned several pieces, one as follows: — "The north wind doth blow, And we shall have snow; And what will the robin do then poor thing? He'll sit in a barn and keep himself warm, And hide his head under his wing poor thing. The north wind doth blow, and we shall have snow, and what will the swallows do then poor things? O, why don't you know they've gone long ago? to a country much warmer than ours poor things. The north wind doth blow, and we shall have snow: and what will the children do then poor things? When school time is done the'll jump, skip, and run; and play till they make themselves warm poor things". I was at singing classes taught by Alexander Brown senior, precentor Auchterless, as also by James Watt, a one armed man a successor of Alex. Brown's, who earned a living by teaching music. Many years after I joined a class of the late John Cheyne's, but he used the sol fa notation and I preferred the staff. I after a few night's practice, paid for the full term and let a little girl anxious to join, fill my place, and finish it.

I never got into a higher arithmetic book at this school, as I left before I was 11 years old. The following lines, sung to C.M. tunes, long, long ago, seem to me to be a fitting finis at this period of life's reminiscences — viz.

> "One year begins, another ends,
> Our time doth pass and go,
> All this for our instruction tends;
> If we could take it so".

AN APPRENTICE TAILOR

I now come to another turn in life's history. A tailor in our district, wanted an apprentice, and hearing of a lad some miles away, who wanted to learn the tailoring trade, I became the bearer of a letter to his folks stating that this man would take him as an apprentice. I brought word back that he was engaged to a tailor in another district. The tailor's wife remarked that I might come and learn myself. The suggestion seemed to open a way of escape from having to go to school; and so in a short time, from being a scholar, I was an apprentice tailor. There were no sewing machines in country districts in those days, although some tailors in the towns had them; all was hand work. I commenced in August, 1861. I served a short period on trial; then an agreement was made out, by which I had to serve for four years, receiving one shilling per week the first year, two the second, two and sixpence the third, and three and sixpence the fourth; getting my food etc, at home. I got on pretty well; but found all was not smooth sailing here more than at school. I got punished at times for not doing my work properly, once to the effusion of blood. I tried to get home and show my bleeding nose, but was held back, and made to wash my face, and thus obliterate any trace of undue punishment. One day, however, he struck me on the thigh with the board used for pressing clothes on, causing a mark that remained a while. This, and other complaints I was making, led to my leaving his service. By this time I had served a year and a half; and as no convenient place was found where I could serve out my time, I was put again to school — not to Gariochsford, but to Ythanwells, the late George Davidson being then schoolmaster there. I cannot write in too complimentary terms of Mr Davidson as a teacher. Apart from his abilities in that respect, he took a great interest in his pupils; getting up games for us in playtime, taking part in them and furnishing at his own expense most of the apparatus required. When I came under his tuition he was unmarried but soon after he married and Mrs Davidson was as much esteemed in the district and by the scholars as was her husband. I got on better at this school than at Gariochsford, though at times I was punished both for neglecting my lessons, as well as for other causes. Mr Davidson did not use the "tag" unduly; but when he did use it, it usually was with marked effect. Cricket was one of our games, and while playing at it one day, a lad, John Milne, and I cast out. He said that the ball struck the wickets, this I denied. He took the bat from me and I retaliated by striking him on the leg with a wicket. This made him cry, and Mr Davidson coming on the scene, both of us were sent into the school, to await our trial: when both were found guilty, and both punished, I being the worst offender getting most. The lad and I were quite friendly afterwards, the feud being but of a transitory nature. I again got punished but the offence was of a less serious nature. A boy, James Forbes, just as our class was to be dismissed, asked me if I would like up the world or down; not knowing what he meant, and thinking it better to get up than down, I replied "up the world"; and got an upward blow on the chin with his book; had I said "down", the blow would have been on the crown of my head. Anxious to try this on someone, I accosted James Duguid sitting in front of me, who, gazing into space was to all appearance oblivious of his whereabouts. The class was dismissed, there was a patter of feet, so taking advantage of this I put the up or down the world question to him, who, all-forgetful of his being in school, cried "No" as loud as he could bawl, making the school sound again. The master looked round in surprise, and inquired who made that noise. Several voices cried out "James Duguid" and presently James was called up to the desk. On being questioned about the noise he had made, he replied that I had asked him if he would like up the water or down the water; (owing to the noise he had indistinctly heard what I had said). His answer seemed to throw no light on the matter, so I was called up. Profound silence now reigned in the school. When asked what I had done to James, to cause him make such a noise, I said I did "nothing", but even this did not satisfy, and so the strap was made use of, and we went back to our seats with different feelings than when we left them. James told me that he forgot he was in the school. On another occasion I got a severe box on my ear, and was sent into the school during the dinner hour. Football was one of our games, and not satisfied with kicking the ball with our feet, we furnished ourselves with sticks to strike it with. Mr Davidson did not approve of this, lest we should hurt each other. None of us, however, understood his remarks as prohibitive, or I am certain we would have obeyed at once. I was the first one he saw using a stick, hence my receiving the above punishment. When the scholars were called in, he emphasized his previous remarks, giving explicit orders that the using of sticks was to be given up at once, and sent out James Massie, Heathfield, Peter

Forsyth, Bogton, and myself to collect all the sticks on the playground, and put them into the stable loft. That we did, staying out a good while, gathering all the sticks we could see, big and little. These were all the punishments I got; except being kept in at times, and once getting my book pitched at me, and told to go to my seat and learn my lesson properly.

OTHER SCHOOL INCIDENTS

One day I managed to answer all the questions put to me, correctly, while another, almost a man, failed, and had to stay in. He knowing that I too would have failed, had certain questions that fell to him been put to me, accused the master of showing me favour and, but for this, I too should have been bearing him company as a defaulter. I was a good distance from the school, when someone came after me saying I was wanted back. I cheerfully returned to find my class-fellow disputing with the master and still charging him with his partiality towards me. A few questions were put to me but, alas, I failed to answer correctly and so my friend went away, feeling that he had won the day. Nothing of this kind ever occurred again. Strange to say, this was the only pupil of Mr Davidson's who in after years spoke disrespectfully of him in my hearing. One day our dictation exercise had the word "know" in it, which I spelled correctly, but on glancing at Isaac Troup's slate who was next me, I saw he had spelled it "no". I took the liberty to copy off him, thinking he would be right. Our lesson finished, we exchanged slates, each correcting his neighbour's one, as the master spelled the words. When he came to the word "know", he said, "Those who have n, o, mark it two errors". So my copying brought its due reward. One lesson taught me at this school, I never forgot, like the knife one at Gariochsford, it came to stay. In our quiet humble rural district, we didn't trouble to being mannerly, at home or elsewhere, to uncover our heads when we entered a house. One day, Mr Davidson took me into the kitchen where I had to wait till he brought a book to me from another room. On his return he found me waiting with my bonnet on, which he took off putting it into my hand, and saying "Robert, I thought you had known better". I did not, but I never forgot.

Mr Davidson had the "knack" of making us interested in
our lessons. We took numbers, and these were entered in a
register, and if we were absent we had to go to the foot of
the class, and work our way up; but, if nearing an examination
time, we did not go to the foot, an average of a week's numbers was taken and these we got instead. In the Bible class I
was from 3 to 6, occasionally no. 1 or top. One thing we did
after reading the lesson, and answering on it was to put questions to those above us, bearing upon what we had been
reading for the past weeks or months. This was an easy way
to get up with a leap, being possible to ask questions one
might not always have at their "finger-ends". Once a big girl
was put to the bottom of the class for misbehaviour. A big
lad wrote a question and answer on a slip of paper which was
passed down to her unseen by the teacher. The question was
put to the one at top of the class, (who was the sender) and
as no one answered it, she got from bottom to top at a bound.
Two lads usually changed places at the lower end of the class;
if Alexander was foot today William would be there to-
morrow. They rarely sought to get further up, the one at the
bottom usually putting his question to his neighbour. Once
Alexander put a question to William that made the teacher
look a little surprised, but when appeal was made to chapter
and verse, the lads were found to be correct. The question
asked was "What did Ishmael do before he died?" William
promptly replied, "Gave up the ghost". Mr Davidson motioned
to the questioner to give the correct answer and take him
down but Alexander's reply was, "He is right". And so he
was, for on turning to Genesis xxv. 17 we read, "Ishmael
. . . gave up the ghost and died".

April 1st 1864 was the annual examination day, con-
ducted by ministers from Forgue, Auchterless, and Drumblade. I got two book-prizes that day, one for letter writing,
the other for English grammar. We were expected to have on
our best clothes. I had a neighbour's jacket on, my own one
being rather shabby, and that was not the only time I appeared
in public in "borrowed plumes".

One afternoon Mr and Mrs Davidson went to Huntly,
leaving us in charge of Willie Nicol, almost a man; he managed
fairly well, although the behaviour at times was not the best.
The arithmetic book some of us had, was a small one, and
had answers to the sums, so we knew when they were correct.
There was one answer, however, to a sum in Compound Pro-
portion, that was wrong. We knew this, but William didn't,

so a few of us pretended to have stuck with this question, and we applied to William for help. This was willingly given us; he showed how to state it etc., but still the answer did not correspond with that given in our book. He now took us up to the black-board where it was worked by him who, by this time looked like, and had assumed all the authority of a fully and duly qualified teacher, but with no better results. After several vain attempts it was given up, and we were sent to our seats, William remarking, that there was a mistake some-where, although he could not find it out. We could have told where the mistake was but as that would have spoiled the programme we kept silent.

My school days terminated in May 1865. This gave me fully 2 years at this school; but as I had to be at home during part of this period, owing to my mother's illness and death it makes it less than two years. When I went to this school, I was the only one from Balgaveny side but before I left there were over a dozen, chiefly owing to Mr Davidson's fame as a teacher. He died in 1904, and Mrs Davidson in 1921. In a newspaper notice (hereafter produced), it was stated that he "was appointed to the teaching staff at Ythanwells". This to me seemed misleading, he being the only teacher, any assist-ance he got was from his older pupils, who taught the junior classes at times. Mrs Davidson proved a great help; not only teaching the little ones, but also the girls sewing. I had some classes to look after, in return for which I got my learning gratis. The following is the newspaper notice referred to. viz. —

"A RETIRED SCHOOLMASTER"

"The death occurred yesterday of George Davidson retired schoolmaster, 83 Beaconsfield Place, Aberdeen. The deceased, who was 66 years of age, was very well known in the north, as he took a keen interest in educational matters, being for some time president of the Aberdeen Branch of the Educational Institute of Scotland. Mr Davidson was a native of Kincardine O'Neil and received his elementary education at Slains Public School. Afterwards he studied at Aberdeen university for some time. He then proceeded to Germany, and was engaged teaching in a private institute. On returning to this country, Mr David-son was appointed to the teaching staff at Ythanwells, Public School, a post which he held for five years. He afterwards occupied a similar position for short periods at Inverkeithney and at Auchterless. Leaving the latter place, Mr Davidson

studied for a time in London, and subsequently was for a time
engaged in teaching at Frankfort on Main. From Frankfort
he proceeded to Paris, and was for a time engaged teaching
private pupils. After staying two years in the French capital,
Mr Davidson was appointed headmaster at Fintray Public
School, a post he held until three years ago, when he retired
on account of ill health. After his retirement Mr Davidson
came to reside in Aberdeen. The deceased was married, and
leaves a widow and one daughter".

Many years after, I went to this school for a short period.
The old faces had disappeared. The teachers were highly respected and I doubt not did their work well, yet I did not
approve of their methods, compared with those of former
years. There was no taking each other down in the various
classes; each one stood up near to where they sat and remained, the class having neither head nor foot.

I now give a description of the school as it was in the
days of my youth, and for many years subsequent, as given
by my respected friend, Mr James Alexander, Post Office,
Ythanwells.

THE SCHOOL

"The school was a modern building, having been built in the
forties of last century, well built, with plastered walls and
slated roof, and well lighted by four or five large windows.
There was one room only, and that was not a large one, but
every inch of available space was occupied as seating room for
children. The school as it is now, consists of two rooms, both
larger than the original schoolroom, yet in the one room were
accommodated a larger number of pupils than the average
attendance of the present day. One gable of the school faced
the west and here the fireplace occupied the centre, with the
schoolmaster's desk at one side, and a short seat and desk for
scholars on the other side of the fireplace. At the opposite end
of the room the door-way occupied a corner and this led into a
small lobby which served the double purpose of class-room
prison cell for minor offenders. Desks were affixed to the walls
all round the remaining wall spaces, and in the centre of the
room desks and seats were so placed as to leave a clear passage
all round the room for the teacher and the pupils to walk up
and down with ease. Between the fireplace and the central
desks there was a clear space in which classes stood during the

lesson hour, and here a piece of ordinary wire had been stapled down to the floor in a semi-circular fashion so that all classes might toe the line during the repitition of lessons. This is a description of the school into which I was ushered before an Education Act or a School Board had been heard of in our rural retreat".

FROM SCHOOL TO FARM

I entered the service of Mr William Robertson, Mains of Hassiewells, at Whitsunday, 1865. He was a widower, and in middle life. His mother, about 80, lived there, also a daughter, just recovering from a long and severe illness. John Ross from Speyside was foreman, and had £10 of fee for the six months. Lewis Harper from Bridge of Dyce, was second, and had a pound less, while his brother John, an old schoolmate, was orra loon, and had considerably less; and I as herd boy got the modest sum of 30 shillings. I must not forget our domestic servant, Helen Reid, hailing from Corse of Kinnoir. In harvest we had three extra hands, a man and two women; viz. Charlie Smith, Hillhead, Aucharnie, able for any kind of harvest work; and B. Smart and M. Deans, from Marnoch, to gather; there was no word of reapers then, all scythe work. That summer was a dry one, a boon for herds, and the harvest was both early and short, being finished in about three weeks. It was a short crop too. I take the following from a letter written to a friend by me while at Hassiewells, and dated 18th September. "We have got all the corn cut, and about half in. John Wood, Lenshie, has got it all in and started the plough". This was a one pair place which in after years was added to the already large farm of Mid Lenshie.

THE HORSEMAN WORD

One evening the second horseman sent me to the shop for a loaf and a candle; as darkness approached, it became evident that something unusual was on the move as men from the adjoining farms called, and an effort was made to get clear of us

two chaps. To effect this the foreman conveyed a neighbour
homeward a short distance taking us with him. We had gone
but a short distance when he said he would go back to his
bed as he felt sleepy. Taking us to the stable he left us, while
he went to the lower end of the steading where he said someone was moving about. John now informed us that he thought
his brother was to get the "horseman word", and we would
not go to bed, but wait and go down to the mill and perhaps
get information. We lay down in the stable; soon after the
foreman entered and, quietness prevailing, left again supposing
us to be in bed and asleep. Not so however. We looked out
and saw men going to the mill below the steading. We followed
stealthily, and went round to the mill-wheel, but were none
the wiser. After a time we ventured to the door, but by this
time Lewis had been initiated into the mysteries of the "horseman word", as they were having a talk upon general topics.
We went to bed, leaving the others to follow when they
thought fit. Next day John told his brother that we and
others had been at the mill and had seen and heard what took
place. This caused annoyance to the men, more so, as I, in-
structed by my companion, gave corroborative evidence.
That night, John being from home, I was taken into the
"chaumer" which was totally darkened, and a book produced,
out of which a few sentence were to be read and then terrible
to relate, his Satanic Majesty would appear and I be left with
him alone in the dark. I was brave, "Yet to my heart, the life
blood went with sudden start", for had I not read a poem by
Robbie Burns telling how an exciseman had been carried
away by the same personage, this being emphasised by a
woodcut showing how it was gone about. If he could carry
away an exciseman, what might he not do to a herd guilty of
falsehood! I was advised to tell the truth and so avoid the un-
desirable alternative. After a little consideration, I made a
clean breast of it, telling them that only John and I were at
the mill, and we heard and saw nothing, beyond hearing them
talk upon general topics.

The book referred to was not one to be dreaded, being an
exposition of the Miller and Horseman words; this I learned
afterwards. I had heard of sounds, and lights, and other
strange things, called into effect by means unknown to me,
and might not this book be one for that very purpose? Hence
my apprehension.

This reminds me on another lad who was fee'd at Mrs
Taylor's, Hassiewells. He went to the tailor's shop on the

other side of the burn, to spend the evening and proposed leaving again about nine o'clock. The tailor was busy, and had to work till the morning hours, to fulfil an order he had on hand. When he was leaving, the tailor, anxious to retain his company, looked out and said that he saw "dead candles" going about the premises at Hassiewells. This was enough for the poor lad who was now afraid to venture home. The tailor went to his bed about three o'clock and the lad lay down on his board in front of the window. It was not long until the tailor asked him, what he would think if the Auld Boy, gave a tap on the window, and said "Ironies"? Not waiting to reply, he sprang from the board, and into the bed at the tailor's back, where he lay till five o'clock, when he got home.

I had about 30 cattle to look after; they were put out at six o'clock in the morning taken to the water, and thence to the fields. These adjoined each other, and this was a boon to me. I had corn on one side and turnips on the other. It took two hours to get to the level at the top of the fields. There I was out of sight, and got a fine view of the surrounding country; and I often saw the train passing over an embankment at Rothievale to Rothienorman about 8 o'clock, my only timepiece. I mind on July 28th: as it was the day Dr Pritchard was hanged at Glasgow for poisoning his wife. I saw the train and knew what would be taking place in Glasgow, where Calcraft would be performing his grim work. Going to the end of the field I moved alongside the marsh between Logie-Newton and Hassiewells, and turned homewards on the other side of the fields, arriving at my starting point about 11, when the cattle were put into the byres till 3 o'clock, when they were again turned out, and the same ground gone over until 8 o'clock, when they were housed for the night. This routine went on day after day, till the beginning of November when the herding ended and the cattle fed in the byres. Herds sometimes fell asleep at their posts; I never had the misfortune to do that. When Martinmas came I left, and went to Skatebrae for orra loon, my wages being £2.2s, and something added to it at the term, if I did the "richt get"; seemingly I had, as this promise was made good. The family consisted of Mr and Mrs Sandieson, two sons, two daughters, and a motherless boy, 5 or 6 years old — a relative they kept. I was as one of themselves, well looked after, never allowed to go from home except on a lawful errand, and not that without asking permission, which was readily granted. Mr Sandieson was an elder in the Episcopalian church at Auchterless,

teaching a class in the Sunday school there, and also holding
a Sunday school in his kitchen on Sunday afternoon. I question if anyone ever filled his place. The following is on a
stone in the churchyard, Auchterless —

> "Erected by Alexander Sandison Farmer, Skatebrae, in memory
> of his daughter Janet who died 19th May 1862 aged 21 years.
> His daughter Elizabeth who died 2nd November 1876 aged 24
> years. The above Alexander Sandison died 15th August 1879
> aged 71 years. His son George died 18th August 1879 aged 24
> years. His son William died 10th March 1892 aged 45 years.
> Elizabeth Robertson wife of the above Alexander Sandison
> died 7th November 1893 aged 75 years. Their daughter Jane
> who died 2nd September 1906 aged 62 years".

George was the first schoolmaster at Birkenhills, Turriff.
I do not know what became of the boy, then known as
"Doodles", but the above shows that I alone remain of the
others — all gone, ALL FILED ON THROUGH THE
NARROW AISLE OF PAIN.

In addition to attending to the cattle, I had to groom,
and work an old mare. Old "Bess" was about 30 years old,
and was easily managed. At Old Yule Mr Sandison paid a visit
to friends in Forgue, and I had to meet him with the old
mare on his homeward journey. It was very frosty, but only
in shaded places was the road slippery. All went well till I
reached the Den of Largue (well known for its frosty condition when other parts of the road is clear), when down
went poor "Bess" with me sitting on her side instead of her
back. I got her up again, but did not venture on to her back.
It was not long till my master appeared so my mind was set
at ease. He had seen the road on daylight, but expected to be
farther on ere he met me. There was work I had to do which
I willingly would have dispensed with, that was wisping straw
as it came from the mill. It was short owing to the dry summer
and not good to do. Besides this work was new to me having
never done it before but I struggled away. It was during this
six months that a disease broke out among the cattle called
rinderpest, for which great precaution was taken and re-
strictions put in force to prevent it from spreading.

It was while I was here that I was at a concert and lecture
on music in the Episcopalian Church, Auchterless. The late
William Carnie, editor of the Northern Psalter, lectured and
pieces were sung by members of the Choral Union, Aberdeen.

There was a harmonium, which was played by W. Morrison, a native of Rothievale, who died in 1922. This was the first time I heard a harmonium. Once I had heard a piano in Huntly, and an organ in St. Margaret's, Forgue. Among other pieces sung was the Hallelujah Chorus, and a hymn to a tune said to be the oldest known sacred tune. I forgot the name but many years after, I made enquiry through the press and was informed it was "Innocents". I expect I got my ticket, or I would not have got it, as pocket money was an unknown commodity to me in those days.

There was a disturbing element manifested itself throughout the evening, which caused Mr Gray to speak out, but he seemed inclined to tholl, rather than use sterner measures.

About 1860 part of the land of Balgaveny was bought by a Mr Petrie, who soon after built a mansion house, where he and a sister lived for some years. He was much addicted to drink, getting so bad at times as to be spoken of as, "The wud [mad] laird o' Balgaveny". The result was that in a few years the estate changed hands. But to return. This laird, who was on a visit to an Auchterless farmer, came to the concert drunk, and made a noise amusing some and annoying others. He told Mr Carnie that he was a better singer than a speaker. The choir was led by Mr Carnie, who compared himself to a traveller carrying samples of his goods, so he by the pieces sung was giving the audience samples to illustrate his lecture; when he mentioned samples, Mr Petrie cried "swatches like". And so the evening passed away and the programme ended.

FROM FARM TO WORKSHOP

Whitsunday, 1866 came, and having put in a year at farm work I again tried the tailoring, and got in at Mr Webster's, Balgaveny. George Munro was cutter and foreman, and John Fraser was journeyman. This brought me again under "the old roof-tree" at night; the bargain being so much money and lodge at home. I made fair progress; having always done some sewing while at school and farm, I had not forgotten my lessons of the past.

I engaged all harvest to Mr Robert Webster, Nether Aucharnie. There were two, at times three scythes. I was raker, and during the leading and finishing up, had to make myself generally useful. My fee was £1.10s, and a good coat, too little

for a son a schoolmaster [?]. Harvest past, I resumed tailoring,
but in the spring of next year while at my work, one who sat
near me, as a lark, gave my head a sudden press down, remarking that I was very earnest. I felt something give a jerk
near the top of my spine, but thought little of it meantime.
However, it was the beginning of an illness that put me from
working for many months, and from the effects of it I never
wholly got over; some blamed the harvest work for it, but I
believe the real cause was as stated above, although out of
deference to my friend, who meant no harm, I said nothing. I
was medically treated, bled with leaches, blistered, drugged
and so forth, but all seemingly to no advantage. It was about
this time that a Mr McConnachie, near Aberlour, had gained a
name as a specialist for dislocated joints, sprains, and such
likes. To him I was taken, [and] under his treatment I slowly
improved. During convalescence Mr Webster took me into the
grocery shop, where I weighed goods for his cart and otherwise helped. A woman of the wandering class came in one
day and among other goods, asked for a pennyworth of tea.
Not finding the small weight used for orders of this nature, I
did what I had seen others do, viz., use a larger one and give
scrimp [short] weight. The old lady, who had been keeping
her eye upon me called out "a' my man you're no givin' me
weight". This brought Mr Webster on the scene who now
served her dealing out a smaller allowance than I was to allow
her remarking that "instead of cheatin' her, I was too liberal".
So she went quietly away and business went on as usual.

After a time I resumed tailoring work, and in December
1868 I finished my apprenticeship; I have already mentioned
some incidents connected with this period of my life. There
is however, a new friend whom I must now introduce. My
sympathy went out to him, for to a certain extent he took
the place that previous to his coming I had occupied. Many
congregated in our workshop in the evenings; frequently my
master would ask them if they ever heard the story about this
lad, pointing to me. The answer would be in the negative, he
then told some terrible exploit, in which I was the chief actor,
and which never took place. When narrated, there were roars
of laughter, which I felt to be at my expense; I laughed to,
and so the effect was better than if I had got angry as has
happened under similar conditions.

This friend, Alexander Paterson, came from Longmanhill,
near Macduff, where his father lived, who was a tailor and
dancing-master, as well as a composer of dance music.

Alexander seemingly "was a chip off the old block", being a tailor, musician, and to some extent, a dancing-master. He was nicknamed "Barney", a name he answered to with all good feeling; he, as already stated, became the "but" of banter instead of me; but it was not this that drew us together: he had a manner about him that made me love him as a very brother; and I do not think I only had this feeling. Like myself he did not drink intoxicants, but one day a plot was hatched that compelled him to purchase a gill of whisky. Day after day he had been pressed to give the others a dram, but refused. The druggist had to act a part in the plot, by suggesting to "Barney" that instead of whisky to offer George "a fissing drink" into which he would put an ingredient to cause a wee bit of annoyance, and still do no harm. Unaware of a plot, George was offered the "fissing drink" which he would thankfully receive although he would have preferred something stronger. The drink was swallowed. There was nothing wrong with it, but, George soon lay down, complaining of severe internal pain, and groaning to an almost alarming extent, remarking that if he did not get a turn soon he could not stand it long. The druggist now appeared, and with great earnestness assured George that the drink was all right and that it was not the cause of his trouble; then taking "Barney" aside, he informed him that a glass of spirits would put George all right: this was soon procured, my friend helping the poor suffering man (?) to sit up, so as to have more freedom to take the remedy. The contents of the glass soon disappeared, but not before George had proposed a toast in keeping with the circumstances. John got a share of the gill, and George began to sew as if nothing out of course had occurred. "Barney" looked on in mute surprise, and I do not think he ever knew how he had been tricked. I saw him in Macduff some years after he left Balgaveny, then I lost all trace of him until 1890, when the following paragraph in a paper met my view.

"Banffshire Captain Drowned. — A telegram has been received from the owners of the Aldergrove, of Liverpool, stating that the captain of that vessel, Alexander Paterson, Macduff, and two of the crew were washed overboard and drowned when the vessel was on a voyage from Sydney to New Caledonia."

I made enquiry, and found that captain Alexander Paterson was my old friend of long ago. "BARNEY".

James T. Shepherd after being several years with Mr

Webster, went to Corse, Forgue, and for several years he
carried on business successfully, as druggist and general merchant; but, like others mentioned, he too was drowned. It was
during the severe snow-storm, in February 1881, on his return from Huntly that he had lost his bearings and having left
the road had fallen into a stream that was filled with "slush",
and perished. He was well known over a wide district, highly
respected, and a general favourite by all who knew him. He
and I once met in a Hawkhall market, where a "cheapjohn"
was busy, trying all and sundry to deal with him. You felt
certain you saw money put into a piece of paper, but no
sooner had a purchase been made than lo it had vanished,
leaving the purchaser a poorer and perhaps wiser man. James
risked giving one pound for what he offered, which looked
large. I gave the pound to the man and handed what I got in
return to James. There was a gather round to see it opened,
that he did with caution, only to find that he had been
"done". He made on that he had the money all right, but
someone in the crowd who saw it opened, cried out, "there's
nae poetry on poun' notes". The papers had poems on them
of a tantalizing nature. It was but a few minutes when a
farmer from Inverkeithnie lost a pound in similar fashion, but
to give him a chance to retrieve his loss he seemingly wrapped
the pound in a piece of paper, and this he offered to him for
a half-crown: this the man gave, but the paper contained only
three pence. Then the man in order he said "to show that he
was really what he professed to be", put a half-crown into a
bit of paper offering it for the three pence. But alas, upon the
paper being opened, no money was in it: others were induced
to deal, and were losers, as no bait was offered, as I have seen
done by that fraternity, as an inducement to deal. Mr Shepherd is interred in Forgue churchyard.

THE HAWKHALL MARKETS

It is long since they were abolished; three being held
annually. The first on the third Tuesday of April, old style
(Pasch Fair). The second on Thursday before the last Saturday of May old style (St Margret's); and the third on third
Tuesday of September old style (Michael Fair). This market
was known to the young folks as the "apple market". The

stance is now mostly under cultivation and added to an adjoining, and already large farm.

A man in our district went to all these markets, besides many others. On one occasion he had bought a stirk, for which he paid 8 or 9 pounds, but forgot all about the transaction. On his return home he discovered that he had lost his money, but how or where he knew not. An old woman, Nannie Horne, who lived a few miles away, was called in, she being supposed able to unravel mysteries by studying the tea-grounds in a cup. Nannie said that the money had been stolen, and there was a woman connected with it, but beyond this she could say nothing. The man's daughter expressed herself satisfied with Nannie's divination which she doubted not was correct. The mystery, however, was solved when a man made his appearance with a stirk. So, however true Nannie's divinations may have been at other times, she certainly erred on this occasion.

COLONEL SHAND'S MONUMENT, FORGUE

Many years ago I wrote to the Huntly Express, calling attention to the above, then much in need of an overhaul. I don't know the effect that may have had on anyone, but I was pleased to see my suggestions as made in the following letter, afterwards carried out.

"SIR, — Would you kindly place at my disposal a small portion of your space in order that I may ventilate a few thoughts that have been passing through my mind of late, and bring them under the notice of your readers, with regard to the above well-known pyramid erected to the memory of Col. Shand on a small eminence overlooking the historic and interesting howe of Frendraught. Col. Shand was a native of the "kingdom," being born at Parkdargue in 1731. Having received a good education, he joined the Royal Regiment of Artillery, was wounded at the battle of Brandywine River in America in 1777, and was present at the memorable siege of Gibralter, 1780-82, where he rendered distinguished service under Lord Heathfield, etc. According to Jervise he discovered and wrote an account of the Roman encampment at Glenmailen, he having occupied a portion of his time with subjects of antiquarian interest. He also did much to improve his estate of Templand, where he died in 1803, and was buried in the churchyard of Forgue, a small monument with a slab built into it marking his resting-place there.

My object in writing is to bring before your readers, especially those who interest themselves in matters relating to the "kingdom," the condition of both monuments which would be greatly improved by being cleaned and repointed, the tables (of which there are three in the pyramid) being to some extent mossgrown. Might not a small sum be collected, and the whole overhauled by some practical tradesman, and so put in a more fitting condition to perpetrate the memory of one who in his day and generation "did his duty," as also to save it from becoming to future generations little better than an antiquarian puzzle, like many relics of the past whose inscriptions have become well nigh, and in some cases altogether effaced by the hand of time? — I am, sir, Yours etc., —

A NATIVE

A JOURNEYMAN TAILOR

As already stated, I finished my apprenticeship in December 1868, and entered the employment of John Reid at the Kirton, Inverkeithnie. The Kirton consisted of the following houses. The manse and offices, and nearby the kirk and kirkyard; kirk and manse are now rebuilt. Then there was the school and schoolhouse; Mr Davidson from Ythanwells being teacher. James Walker tenanted the shop and post office. James Garden, formerly at Aucharnie, was shoemaker; and John Reid with whom I worked was tailor. The farm of Mansefield was held by an old man Gordon, author of a once popular song, about a lass he met "upon sweet Ythan side". Other two houses were occupied by labouring people. This compact hamlet is pleasantly situated on the Keithnie near to where it joins the Deveron. Soon after I went there considerable alarm was caused by "lichts" being seen in the kirkyard, when one was near the manse. Mr Souter, the minister, said that it was probably caused by phosphorus coming from a newly opened grave; this however did not satisfy the curious. The light was being talked about in our workshop one night, when it was suggested that we might go to the kirkyard and try to solve the systery. This was done: I was one of the company. The light was only seen from a certain place, we took a straight course from this to near the middle of the kirkyard. This caused us to go over the dyke, instead of keeping the path and entering by the gate. I was careful not to be the first nor the last to go over the dyke, supposing that safety lay in being in the middle. When we were well into the kirkyard it was soon seen what had caused the alarm.

The boatman across the Deveron, who was also a shoe-maker, had newly erected a wooden workshop, the light from which shining on a polished gravestone had caused the alarm. Similar occurrences take place. I remember once seeing a light that gave me a surprise. It was dark, and the snow fell gently in large flakes, causing uneasiness when they fell on the face. I wore a pair of woollen mittens, and frequently wiped my face with them to remove the flakes from my eye-lids; when all at once a spark of light appeared at each finger-tip, shone for a few seconds, and then vanished. About the same time I saw by the papers that a similar thing happened at Fisherford, it being the man's whiskers in this instance that were involved; and I had a similar experience many years sub-sequent. I can give no explanation of this.

At Whitsunday, 1869, John Reid went to Bridge of Forgue, as tailor and cutter to Alexander Stewart, merchant, and I went with him. He and his Mrs were well known and had a good name over a wide and extended district. He was a carpenter and farmer, as well as merchant and postmaster. He rented a small farm at Muirton, there toiling all day, and assisting in the shop at night, where Mrs Stewart, (familiarly known as "Bell o' the Brig") had been busy all day. Sandie told me years after that it would have been better had he let the farming alone, and devoted his attention to the shop. I was at the Brig for about 3 years, but partly under another cutter, as John Reid went to Balgaveny.

I narrate a few incidents of this period. James Napier came at a busy time as a journeyman, he served his time with Joshua M'Kenzie, Gordonstone, Auchterless, with whom I worked in 1875 and '6. James was very nice, and we got on without friction and, in after years when we met we looked back with pleasant recollections. One night I played him a trick, which he enjoyed, although it deprived me of ever being similarly employed by him. James was to visit a girl one night, after the others were in bed. There was a risk of his

being caught unawares at a certain corner, hence my being
taken along to act as guard. I let him tap at the window, and
then threw a stone that alighted near him. This led him to
come to me to enquire if I had seen or heard anything. I said
that I heard something like a stone going down the close.
James left me to watch at the upper end of the house while
he looked round the lower. I let him go a short distance, and
then I flung a stone after him, and said "ther's nae dou't but
that's a stone". He took to his heels, sprang over fences like a
deer, I followed as fast as possible; when a good distance
from the house he halted and helped me over a dyke. I then
told him who threw the stones, but he did not venture to go
back again that night.

When work got slack James had to leave, and when the
busy time came again, and trade revived, his place was filled
by one Archie Stables, from Aberchirder. Archie's father was
a tailor and he had learned with him. He was at the "Brig"
the Summer that Donald Dinnie first appeared at Huntly at
games. There was a great gathering from the surrounding
districts. They were held in the Castle Park. Sandie Stewart
took a cartload of us, and Archie went up to take the first
prize for running, telling us as we went up that if he did not
get in first he would let the one who did so know what he
was running for. But better runners were there and Sandie
Stewart remarked, "Oor Archie's gotten the privilege o'
comin' in hin'most". Archie ran well, he could sing, and was
a good player on the flute. I had promised him a drink of
porter if he ran at all, so to fulfil that promise we went to the
inn at Bogniebrae, where two bottles of porter were bought,
and about one and a half consumed; then Archie mixed what
was left with water, filled the bottles poured some into
tumblers, and rang the bell. When the girl came in he asked
what this was she had given us, she said "porter, what was
asked for". She was told to taste it, and said, "its nae verra
gweed"; adding that "it was what she got to give us". Archie
rose in seeming indignation. remarking that he "never was in-
sulted with stuff of that kind", and walking out of the room
turned round at the door saying sharply to me, "Come away,
Robert". I obeyed, and so we left the girl with the porter, and
I do not think we were ever back again. Of course it was paid
for, the sequel being a little joke of Archie's. Afterwards he
joined the army; then resumed tailoring, subsequently married,
seemingly did all right for a time, but gave way to drink, and
he and his wife separated. Years after, an advertisement was

put into the papers inquiring for him, he saw it, and said that an uncle had died abroad leaving him a fortune. On hearing this, some of his old cronies advanced him small sums of money, expecting to be paid back when once the lawyers had gotten his uncle's matters all settled: so he lived gloriously (?) for a short time, but alas it soon became apparent why he had been "wanted". He was divorced. For a short time he was brought prominently before the public, and then vanished from sight. Poor Archie!

The next man at the "Brig" was Peter Meldrum, from Cobairdy, Forgue. His father had a croft, and was sawmiller there. Peter served his time at Kinnoir. He died December 1922 at Aberdeen. We both worked with J. Reid, and his successor Wiliam Smart. We were both at Badenscoth too, but not together. Peter and his father were both good shots. Peter kept his eyes open when he took aim, and he said his father did the same. He was telling how at home, in the clear nights, with snow on the ground he had shot rabbits, so we were to have a trial at it here; we got hold of Sandie Stewart's gun, and ammunition, and about midnight we went out to try our luck among the rabbits. Going to a wood at Mill of Forgue, we sat and watched ever so long, but nothing came within range. Getting cold we removed to near Woodland Cottage, but with no better results. After waiting a while we resolved to go home to bed, and try again so we made for our lodgings at the Muirton. We went by the back of the houses at the "Brig", as had we kept the road and passed at the front, our view of the road was cut off by a hedge, and might meet somebody unexpectedly, and so we got past safely. When about 200 yards past the bridge, we heard voices behind us, and looking round, saw two men crossing the bridge , and listening, heard one of them say, "Een o' them had a gun". We waited to hear no more, but ran home as fast as we could, drew the charge from the gun, put it where we got it, and hurried to bed, resolving that it would be our first and last attempt at night poaching, a resolve kept. We never heard who the speakers were; they must have been in Sandie's orra shed which was open, when we passed. Perhaps we frightened them; they however, did us a turn. The penalty for night poaching at that time was imprisonment without the option of a fine. Peter in a few years commenced working on his own account; finally settling down in Aberdeen, and died as stated above.

It was while working here that I got acquainted with the

late Willie Macraw [?] living then at Hillhead of Frendraught.
On a dark night he came into our shop, under the influence
of liquor, and speaking a good deal, among other things, he
reminded us that he had to pass the "Clatterns", a lonely
spot, having a name for being uncanny. Willie spoke about
the strange sights and sounds to be seen and heard there,
assuring us that at times all the musical instruments mentioned
in the Bible could be heard playing, special mention being
made of the harp, and the piper that played before Moses;
whoever he may have been. Alexander Adam, blacksmith,
Bogniebrae, was present, and as he was going to the Raich he
went over the hill and awaited Willie at the uncanny spot.
Willie arrived: the smith let him past, then gave vent to a
weird cry, Willie stood and listened; again the cry sounded
forth, and without waiting to enquire whether it was the
harper or the piper who had uttered the cry, he ran away as
fast as possible. Willie lived long after this, first at Hawkhall,
and afterwards at Hareness; he died in the Forgue Cottage
Hospital.

It was at this period of my life that a desire got hold
hold on me to learn photography. I paid Mr Bremner, Banff,
two pounds and was with him a month learning. Those were
the days of the wet collodion process, now superceded by
other processes. My term finished with Mr Bremner, I visited
friends in Aberdeen, walked to Stonehaven, paid a visit to
Bervie, Montrose, and other places, including Bridge of Dun
[Forfarshire], where I saw Queen Victoria, the royal train
stopping there a few minutes on the homeward journey from
Balmoral. Funds were now nearly exhausted so I made tracks
for home, arriving there safely but poorer, but otherwise
none the worse of my adventures. I again resumed tailoring
work at Forgue, and so I was there for a while, but after a
time I thought I would be better of a change so as to get
more "insight". With this end in view, I visited Aberdeen in
quest of work, but found the master tailors more concerned
about getting work, than of taking on fresh hands. I went up
Deeside with no better results. I have a good word to say
about the Deeside folks. On the south side of the river I
called at a house, and asked for a drink of water and was
offered milk instead. On the north side, it being now dark,
I called at another to inquire the distance to Banchory, having
got the information asked for, I again went on my journey,
when a man came after me from the house, and inquired if I
was in want of food, as they would give me if I was in need

of it. Not being in need of food I did not accept of their kind offer of hospitality: I often remembered these two proffered acts of kindness shown me in one day, and looked on the Deeside folks as being a nice and kind-hearted people. A similar instance never occurred in my experience in any other district through which I as a stranger passed through. I stayed two days in Banchory, then tramped across the country passing Kincardine O'Neil, Dess, Lumphanan, Alford, and Insch, ultimately landing at Balgaveny, from which I started a week previously; and again found employment at the Bridge of Forgue, where I stayed till the May term, after which I was at Balgaveny again for a short time. When I was at Forgue an incident occurred which I will now relate. I paid a visit to Mr Shepherd at Corse one night, there had been strange things said to be taking place at a croft near Glenfoudland, of a supernatural nature, which led to the talk being a good deal upon "feart things", and it was dark, and I had to go all the way to Forgue alone. I got past the Green Gate at the Corse in safety, past Frendraught and past the last house, and, near-ing the Clatterns, when it came into my head that I might be safer not to go past it, and so I went through the Raich's parks, to the turnpike at the toll-bar and got home all right; I, however, kept this matter to myself.

My next move was to Turriff, getting work from the late James Dawson. I joined the Good Templars while at Turriff, but never got farther than the first degree, as I never after-wards was connected with a Lodge. I had a fellow lodger, by name John Robertson, who worked at the woolmill (now extinct), who in his spare time wrote verses. I too had a try at it, and after a few unsuccessful attempts one very short piece appeared in the People's Journal, and having been thus far successful, I gave it up. It was the shortness of it more than its worth however, that was its chief recommendation, as the following note by the editor shows. "R.B.'s poem is so short that more space would be sacrificed in criticising it and point-ing out its merits and demerits than in putting it in print, so here goes" —

SPRING

Spring once more has sallied forth,
And quelled the cold winds from the north;
Over the mountain, over the plain
Gentle Spring has come again.

It is spreading verdure far and wide,
By the river's marge, and the mountain side;
The birds in the woods now sweetly sing,
To welcome thy coming, O gentle Spring!

The following were among the "declined for various reasons".
[Barclay's verses, entitled 'The Scottish Heather-Bell', 'Old
Scenes Revisited', and 'On Catching a Trout' are omitted.]

.   .   .   .

A friend was going to America, whom I was to say good-
bye to on a certain day. He however, left earlier, and I did
not see him; the salutation I got was, "Jockey's awa' an' ye'll
never see 'im again". Hence the following letter I sent him; he
did come back after many years, and returned to America,
taking some of his friends with him. All the notice that the
editor took of it was to say that sea and America did not
rhyme; but the friend who got it, called me a first rate poet;
so that was some encouragement.

AN EPISTLE TO A FRIEND IN AMERICA

Can it be true, they tell me, That I'll never see you more?
Or hear your voice again, Upon our native shore?
O man! it makes me sorry, When I mind on the days,
The happy days o' boyhood, Wi' a' their childish plays,
When we used to go to school, Or roam beside the wood,
And sport away the moments In fun as best we could;
Ye little thought o' leaving Our humble, native glen,
Or the lowly thackyt cottage, Wi' its 'but' and its 'ben'
But now you are far from them, And soon will be forgot
The place that so well knows you, Will shortly know you not
You've gone to push your fortune, Across the Atlantic Sea,
In the far and distant land, Of north America.
I fancy that I hear thee, Though o'er the rolling sea,
Sighing for the wood and glen, Where once thou wast so free
Yet though we are far severed, O man! I wish you well,
And may you never want a home; Where you may safely dwell.

So here ends my poetical (?) effusions, of which the
above is a sample, enough being as good as a feast I change
the subject.
I worked in Turriff on two different occasions, after

which I was at Balgaveny up till Whitsunday 1873, when a desire to see a little beyond the bounds of my native parish again entered my mind, so I went to Inverness, and stayed there for one night. I would have stayed longer, as I paid for two night's lodgings, but for the following incident. Being tired knocking about, I went early to bed. There was another man in the same room and, after I had been asleep, I was awakened by a second man coming in, and who I was informed was to share my bed. He partook of a hearty meal, and produced some beer, which he was willing to share with us. Being a Good Templar I refused, and had no more trouble, the other gentleman had no scruples, but partook of it rather freely, and in a short time it took so much effect upon him that his tongue refused to go round the words, and he fell asleep. My companion now informed me that he had put spirits amongst the beer, and that was what caused it to have such an effect on our friend. It is in similar circumstances that Good Templarism may prove a help to one, when fairly carried out. I thought it did me a good turn on this occasion. My bed-fellow now came to bed, inquiring into my past life, as well as my purposes for the future, all the time assuring me he had a great interest in my welfare. I being, he said, the one he had been on the outlook for as a companion for a while. He said he was canvassing for maps, etc., soliciting orders from school-teachers, and the upper classes; and as he was going to Beauly on the morrow, and pressed me to accompany him there. I could not make out what part I had to act in the business, but after the beer incident, I resolved to shake myself clear of him. Morning came, but, do my utmost, I could not get away from him, he watched my footsteps, and seemed determined not to lose sight of me. I forget many of the incidents of that morning. After breakfast he wanted me to go into a public house with him; I refused, but was to wait till he came out. As soon as he was inside I bolted, and went to the railway station at hand, and from behind a carriage where I would not easily be seen by one coming into the station, I watched the entrance. In a few minutes my friend appeared, looked around, and not having seen me, went away; and as John Bunyan says, "I saw him no more". I took the train to Lhanbryde, but was not far from Inverness when a man under the influence of strong drink spoke to me in Gaelic, to whom I could not reply in that language. He then said in English, "Can sho no speak the Gaelic?". I told him that I could not, and to this he replied, "I wouldn't give sixpence for a man that can't speak the Gaelic". I made no reply and so our conversation ended. Arriving at Lhanbryde, I walked to Buckie, and got work from Marquis Silverstine, a German Jew who worked chiefly for the fisher folks. I lodged with a relative.

I often thought of my visit to Inverness, and wondered what that man was after, whose demeanour to some extent spoiled my visit to the northern capital. Many of the Buckie fisher folks, as also those in towns and villages along the coast, went to Fraserburgh and Peterhead to follow their calling during the summer; many of the other tradesmen accompanying them carrying on their respective businesses, wherever they went. My master went to Peterhead, and I went too, but it did not turn out to be a profitable speculation for him. All depended on the fishing, whether it was good or bad. If good, there would be plenty of money to put into circulation, making trade brisk; if bad, better stay at home, as rents were high, and the transmission of one's effects cost a good deal. I went to Peterhead in one of the Buckie fishing boats, my first sea voyage. It was very calm yet I was sick for some hours, and having taken no food with me, was rather hungry ere we reached our destination. The fishing over I returned to Buckie, and remained there till the Spring of 1874, when I returned to my old employer John Reid, who had left Mr Webster and was working on his own account at North Balgaveny. I visited Marquis and his wife on several occasions in after years. He died on 26th April 1913. The following appeared in a newspaper.

> "The death occured on Saturday in the Parish Hospital at Buckie of Mr Marquis Silverstine. For the past three years deceased had been unable to work, and had been an inmate of the hospital for about three weeks. A native of Prussia, he came to England over 40 years ago and to Buckie about 30 years ago, and carried on the business of tailor in the Seaton. He became a naturalised British subject, and a convert to Christianity. He acted as church officer in the Free Church (now the South United Free), and soon made his personality felt in the congregation. Becoming a Sunday school teacher, he took charge of a large infant class, and many Buckie people who are now no longer young will remember the early religious instruction they received from Marquis. At picnics and social meetings he was much in evidence superintending the making of the tea, in which he took great pride. A keen politician

with socialistic leanings, he was in the habit of stopping
people of his acquaintance in order to propound some political
theory, or talk about passing events. He was a persistent heckler
of political candidates. He was for a term a member of the
Rathven Parish Council, and his intimate knowledge of the
fisher folk was often of use in deciding cases. A few years ago
disease set in in his foot for which amputation was necessary,
and since then he has been a pensioner of the Buckie Lodge of
Oddfellows. His wife, a native of Buckie, predeceased him
several years ago. He was 67 years of age".

Some years after I left Marquis I was a short time with
George Taylor, the Square, Buckie. Among others in his
employment was a young man, Alexander Griffiths, from
Edinburgh. Afterwards I saw he was found dead at the roadside at a farm, Bogbain, in Morayshire, perhaps another victim
to strong drink.

John Reid married Miss Shand, Yonderbognie, while we
were at the Bridge of Forgue. Previous to his marriage we did
the cooking of our food ourselves, I being principal cook,
and this has proved useful to me in subsequent years.

At Whitsunday 1875 J. Reid went to Aberchirder, he
having been appointed postrunner between that and Bogniebrae, a post he held for many years. I went to Badenscoth,
then occupied by Ross Hunter and Son. John Noble Anderson
was cutter. I was greatly taken up with him, but like many,
he at times was a victim to strong drink, although he kept
steady for a good while on end. He was a very intelligent
man, who had read much, and was willing to impart his
knowledge to others. It was through him that I first heard of
spiritism; as also, the late Dr George Macdonald's religious
teachings. Having read most of his books, he could convey to
anyone willing to listen and learn, the contents and the teachings of the same. I pass over John's shortcomings. After
leaving the district he enlisted, served in the Egyptian war,
and returned to Aberdeen where he married a second time,
subsequently dying there. Many came into our workshop in
the evenings, among others was a blacksmith, who related the
extraordinary doings of a shoemaker at Wartle, Alexander
Henderson, usually called "Skarrie", as he came from the
farm of Skares, Culsalmond. He was a shrewd old man, and
could work on the feelings of the young farm-servant chaps,
who often would consult him on matters relating to horse-
manship. I had often heard of him, and had known of him

being consulted in cases where cows were supposed to have been bewitched, or otherwise tampered with, so as to prevent them from giving milk etc. The smith was telling us one night of his wonderful doings, some awe-inspiring, assuring us that all he told us was fact and were we beside him he would soon give us convincing manifestations of his wonderful powers. I suggested that we might go to his abode, 5 miles distant, and see for ourselves. This was agreed to, and 6 of us set off on foot to see some of the strange doings of "Skarrie". The following made up the company; John Noble Anderson, cutter, Alexander Gillan, Henry Clark, tailors, Alexander Coutts, shop-keeper, John Clark, carpenter, Upperthird, and myself. When we arrived at the old man's humble abode we found it in darkness, but a knock at the door was answered by Sandie's daughter, who upon being informed who we wished to see led us into a closet where her father was in bed with a small dog beside him. John was spokesman and told him that he had brought a few young chaps to him who had been troubled by seeing lights, and hearing strange sounds they could not account for. The old man sat up on his elbow, and fixing his sharp and somewhat piercing eyes upon us informed us that he did not "belong to this century", a remark that seemed to solemnize most of us. He meant that he was born previous to 1801, but it was said in a way as almost made one feel he hinted at something uncanny, nor was this to be wondered at, after all we had heard related concering him, by our friend the blacksmith. He then glanced at us inquiring about the lights. John motioned to the shopkeeper to come forward, at the same time saying, "Ye'll better him Coutts". Coutts was taken by surprise, and scarcely could speak, so after uttering a few stammering words, John to his relief, again became spokesman. Sandie was approached as to his weird performances, but showed us none of them, he said he was willing to help anyone, and would come to Badenscoth the next night, and bring a preparation with him that would dispel both lights and sounds, We now took our journey homeward not much wiser. Sandie dressed and accompanied us a mile; when parting, John put round his hat to take up a small collection for Sandie's behoof. Some had no money. I was asked to put in something for them. I did so, and I fear I never got it all back again, so I had to "pay the piper" for my suggestion to go to Wartle; however the sum was small and learning like pleasure has to be paid for. So we parted, Sandie going home a little richer, and I slightly poorer but

not much wiser. True to his promise, Sandie came to Badenscoth the next night and was ushered into the tailor's shop by
Coutts and I who found him sitting at the roadside near the
shop. A little pleasant talk was engaged in for a short time,
it then turned to the supernatural. John drew "Skarrie's"
attention to a young carpenter, who had been telling us
about lights that had appeared near his father's workshop. He
eyed the lad closely, and then asked for a small phial, this
was handed to him and into it he poured a few drops out of a
bottle he took from his pocket; this he gave to the lad
bidding him empty it at the spot where he saw the light
disappear, at the same time telling him to say words which
I refrain from reproducing, and the lights would give him
no more trouble. The lad did not take the bottle with him
as I found it next morning, behind some boxes. By this
time some strong drink had been imbibed by those who cared
for it, and Sandie was telling of many wonderful things he
could do, but when told to go on and perform he would not.
Among other things, he said that were he to take the roe of a
frog and hold it over the flame of a candle, at the same time
saying a few words over it that he durst not mention, almost
instantly the place would be crawling with living frogs. The
blacksmith assured us all was true, yet Sandie would give no
demonstration to prove his supernatural powers in spite of a
fair amount of coaxing, and so all on a sudden he was put
outside, because he would not give any proof of his alleged
supernatural powers. So our expected entertainment never
came off. Coutts and I accompanied him homewards for some
distance, doing our best to "pour oil on troubled waters",
attributing John's behaviour to the effect of drink, and to the
best of our ability made apology for what had taken place,
and so ended our dealings with "Skarrie". I was in his
house some years after this, but I do not think he knew me,
and I made no reference to the past.

THE TAILOR AND HIS CUSTOMER

In one of the now all but obliterated hamlets, there lived
a tailor and his wife. This "Knight of the Thimble", Charlie
Robb, was noted for being a little slow at executing orders
received for tailor work. A farm-servant, in the district, brought

material to him to make a vest, which was to be made shortly;
but when he called for it, was told to come back as he had
not got it done yet owing to his having so much work on
hand. This went on for some time, until one night the lad
dressed and slightly disguised called on the tailor, saying he
was a journey-man in quest of work, and asked him to take
him on. Charlie's wife told him her husband could not give
him work as he had very little work for himself. So he left,
but the tailor was a wee bit irate when he learned afterward
who the journey-man was; and history is silent as to when the
vest was ready.

Years rolled by. The hamlet was almost obliterated;
Charlie's wife died, and he went to another district, took
unto him another wife, who had a small croft, here they lived
happily for many years. He came to Badenscoth for the harvest while I was there. The "chaumer" accommodation was
limited, so he slept in our bedroom 8 steps above our workshop. Once some of us had to work all night so as to get some
clothes finished by a certain time the next day. A shop-keeper
bore us company until well through the night and there being
two alarm clocks, he kept them sounding every fifteen minutes or so, as long as he stayed, Charlie responding to their
appeals by an occasional groan or a "hoch-hey". When morning came he descended the steps with a look indicating that
he was not in the best of humour. I greeted him with the
salutation, "O happy man that wine to your bed while we
poor chaps maun toll on a' nicht". His response was, "I kenno'
fat better I am o' beddin', fin I didno' get sleep; yon wis a din
at ye raist", at the same time aiming a blow at the side of my
head with his open hand. I evaded the blow, and Charlie went
out to his breakfast and his work, so this incident closed, no
mention ever being made of that alarming night; he and I remained friendly as formerly and I do not suppose he ever
knew how innocent I was as to that night's din. Afterwards I
was near his abode and calling, had my tea with him and his
wife. A few more years passed, and both had gone the way of
all the living. How appropriate are the poet's words!

.   .   .   .

John Anderson was succeeded by William Macrobbie as
cutter. He left and A. Harper came when Mac. left. I was with
both, nice agreeable men. It was Mac. who learned me to cut,
after Harper was away and Mac. back again, and after I was

at Gordonstone.

After being a few years at Badenscoth, Mr Macrobbie went to Aberdeen where he had a business of his own, subsequently dying; his widow survived him for many years, dying in Aberdeen, May 1922.

As stated above, I left Badenscoth in Mr Harper's time and went to Joshua Mackenzie, Gordonstone, who carried on a small tailoring business and sold groceries. The family consisted of husband and wife, two sons, and two daughters; the oldest son was serving his apprenticeship with his father. The house was near to James Beatie's shop where he taught his scholars, and carried on shoemaking too. He was dead ere then, but a son, two grandsons, and a great grandson — then a boy, were alive; all are now dead. The great-grandson died after a short illnesss in the end of 1922, while yet in his prime, leaving a widow and six daughters; so after four James Beaties being here, the name becomes extinct.

The following tribute was paid to Mr James R. Beattie the last of the four, by Mr Scott, United Free Church, Auchterless. — "Mr Beattie came of a family that was well known far beyond the bounds of the parish. He was greatly respected — and justly so, for he was a man of strict integrity and high moral character. He was of a lovable disposition. He had a kind word for everyone, and spoke evil of no one. It was a great pleasure to be in his company and enjoy fellowship. Those who knew him could tell how varied were his interests. Nothing human was foreign to hm. He was a quiet man, who read much and thought much. Although interested in the work of the congregation, he did not see his way to accept office, although elected again and again. He will be missed in the congregation and in the parish, but most of all in the home. Sympathy is expressed for his widow and family in their bereavement".

It was while working at Gordonstone that I became acquainted with the late James Simpson, who with his wife and others were killed in China by the Boxers, in July 1900. James belonged to the Belhelvie district, but had many relatives I knew in Forgue. He was a journeyman tailor at Badenscoth for some time; after which he was a steward on a steamboat, plying between London and Aberdeen for a few weeks. I next came across him as cutter and tailor to a merchant in Insch. I think he was married by that time. I lost sight of him for many years, but during this time he and his wife had been in China as missionaries in connection with the China Inland

Mission. We again met in 1894 when he and his wife were
home on furlough. Soon after they returned to China, labouring in another mission, under a Pastor Pigott at Shanyang etc.
While there we kept touch by post up to near their martyrdom.
Many of other missions were killed at this time.

. . . .

I stayed with Mr Mackenzie till May term, 1877; he died
2nd October of that year, aged 55, and James his youngest
son died some years later, a young man of 19. Mrs Mackenzie
died 15th April 1918, aged 85 years. It was in September
1876 that I took a trip to the Shetland Isles, at least the
capital — Lerwick. This might have been all but forgotten,
had it not been that some years later I contributed a paper on
this subject when a member of A Mutual Improvement Class
at Ythanwells. Other papers were written but this one, and
another on Temperance, alone survive.

A TRIP TO SHETLAND

A day comes once a year, which is usually looked forward to with pleasure. It is talked about for weeks and it may
be for months before hand. It is our "annual holiday". One
asks the other "where are you going to spend it?" Some are
going one way and some another, while many for want of
cash, must stay at home. To those whose time and means
permit, a visit to the Shetland Isles would prove highly
interesting. Those out-of-the-way Isles present features of
interest not to be met with in other parts of our land. It is
true they lack much that is to be seen in other parts of the
kingdom, but this want is supplied to the full by what occu-
pies its place.

I propose taking you, if willing to accompany me, on a
trip to those northern isles. More than one day, however, is
required to go there, not to mention the time we would
need to look about us and return; and yet I must not exceed
20 minutes. Leaving Aberdeen with the steam-boat on Friday
night, we arrive at Lerwick the capital of Shetland early on
Sunday morning; this alone takes 30 hours, while going, visit,
and return must as I have stated, be accomplished in about

20 minutes. If I go beyond that the chairman may be telling me to sit down. To prevent him from having to perform this duty, I will try and not exceed the specified time; endeavouring to interest all, and weary none. Our conveyance is old and swift, being that faculty of the mind we call imagination. With it we can visit the frozen north, and bask in tropical sunshine all in a moment. Man may bind our bodies, if he wills to do so, but who can bind our imaginations? "Free to all men universal prize". Each of us then, may for once in our life ride in our own vehicle, while we take a trip to Shetland. There are two ways of going there, so far at least. We can go per rail to Thurso, cross the Pentland Firth to Orkney, and catch the steamer at Kirkwall going to Lerwick. The alternate route, is direct by steamer from Aberdeen. This we will take, being the cheapest and least troublesome. As we are familiar with most of the places of interest between this and Aberdeen we will pass over this part of our trip. When I visited Shetland I did so rather late in the year. June, July, or August are the best months. My visit was made in September when the weather was rather cold and stormy. A friend in Aberdeen who went to the isles 4 times a year on business, advised me to postpone my visit till next year, and go earlier, he said that I would repent going before I was out of sight of Aberdeen; adding that he expected it would be a rather stormy night: however, I went, and had I not done so, this subject would not have been handled by me, as I have had no opportunity of going in after years. My friend's estimate of the weather was correct.

At the Harbour all is hurry and bustle. The crew of the St Magnus are busy discharging and loading cargo previous to sailing. Friends are saying good-bye to each other, with best wishes for a safe voyage. The scene brings to mind the poet's words, "And there were partings such as crush the life from our young hearts, and choking sighs which ne'er may be repeated, who can tell, if ever more shall meet those mutual eyes?" On the steerage all is neat and clean: a dance is going on to the strains of a violin. My friend advised me to try and fall asleep before sailing, as this might prevent sickness, if I did not waken until we were well out at sea. All efforts, however, to fall asleep proved useless as my eyes refused to be sealed by "balmy sleep", although it was nearly midnight. I thought if the dancing would only stop, I might fall asleep, but then that would be selfish to expect folks to stop their amusements solely for my sake, so I kept silent, thinking it

better that one should be put about rather than many. Soon
the ship began to dance to the music of the waves, which
brought the other music and dancing to a speedy termination.
So softly does it glide along for a short period that some are
in doubts if we have really started on our voyage. All on a
sudden we begin to roll and to toss on the waves, removing
all doubt as to our having started, making one accustomed to
the solid ground, feel a little "out of sorts". Someone explains that we are "crossing the bar". and soon sailing will be
pleasant. To my mind we kept crossing it all the night, and
the sailing was far from pleasant, including the sea-sickness
which effected most of us. Various preventives were resorted
to for this troublesome experience, including the one I used,
chlorodyne, which was useless.

    Next morning, we arrived in Wick Bay, where changes are
effected with both passengers and goods. Those who desire it
can get breakfast, consisting of bread, roast beef, and coffee,
for 1/6: the charge for dinners being 1/9, and tea 1/3, total
4/6, rather more than we usually pay at home, we must bear
in mind, that when bent upon pleasure we must pay for it.
Purchasing food, however, was not compulsory, as you could
take it with you.

    From Wick to Kirkwall the voyage was pleasant and sick-
ness gave me no trouble, which was not the case with many
on board. A glimpse was had of the Orkney Isles as we went
north. Kirkwall was reached at 5 o'clock p.m. on Saturday,
an hour and a half is spent similarly as at Wick, and again we
go northward.

    The fare between Aberdeen and Kirkwall was 8/- single,
15/- return, available for one calendar month. Lerwick is
about 100 miles farther north, yet this only cost sixpence,
return ninepence. Night is now setting in, which prevents us
from seeing the northern isles of the Orkney group. Between
Orkney and Shetland is the Fair Isle, inhabited by about 300
people who chiefly employ themselves at fishing. It has high
hills, and in clear weather is seen from a great distance, but
in fogs it is dangerous. I did not see it, as it was night when
we passed it both ways. On the return voyage, owing to a
dense fog it was necessary to stop and take soundings, I asked
at a lad connected with the boat why we had stopped, and
was told that they were "deepenin' the water". Before we
arrived at Lerwick, we had to go through Sumburgh Roost; a
strong rough current occasioned by the meeting of rapid tides
which flow along each side of the Shetland group. It is about

20 miles broad, and in stormy weather is well nigh impassable, and in moderate weather one may expect a good rocking, although there is no difficulty in getting through it. Large numbers of saithe fish are caught in it. Anchor is cast in the harbour at 3.30 on Sunday morning — a rather untimely hour in a strange land. The boat, whose arrival is announced by the firing of a small cannon, cannot get close to the shore, there being no landing place, but remains 80 to 100 yards out in the harbour; passengers and goods being taken ashore and re-shipped free by the mail-boats, but other boats are near and if you step into any of them you will have to pay the fare.

. . . .

The public buildings in the town [Lerwick] include Fort Charlotte, the Educational Institute, the Widow's Asylum, and 8 or 9 churches etc. I was in 3 of them. In the forenoon I listened to an address on the duty of studying the Bible. In the afternoon a missionary from India gave an account of missionary work in that land, stating some of the difficulties missionaries had to contend with; he said caste distinction was a great hindrance to missionary work in India. In the Congregational kirk at night he again took up this subject giving additional information.

. . . .

About 3 miles from Lerwick I saw a house without a "lum", a hole in the roof served the purpose, out at which the smoke came. Nearby a pig being led with a halter and tethered on a field of grass like a cow, or other animal, and seemingly at home.

I visited the kirkyard of Tingwall, expecting to find some rare inscriptions on some of the gravestones; but was disappointed. I saw at some distance the village of Scalloway which, as before mentioned was once the capital. Near the village is the "Witches' Hill" where in other days those who practised the "diabolical art" were tied to a stake and burned, the last victim being B. Tulloch and her daughter Ellen King. It is pleasant to know that those days are gone by, and witches now a thing of the past. I believe they still exist, but not the old repulsive individuals we often read about or saw in pictures. I would ask one question. If witches are extinct, how is it that so many men get bewitched? "Oh!" says

someone, "It's fine to be bewitched". "What signifies the life
o' man, An' 'twere no for the lasses O".

.   .   .   .

I trust I have wearied none with this trip, and in "case be"
will bring it to a close. So without waiting for the steamboat
we again mount our own vehicle, and casting a glance at these
isles as they rest on the bosom of the "deep blue sea", we bid
them GOOD NIGHT, and next moment find ourselves not in
SHETLAND, but I hope pleasantly and comfortably convened
in the schoolroom at YTHANWELLS.

TOTAL ABSTINENCE VERSUS MODERATE DRINKING

This subject demands cautious handling; for in the heat
of a true and just enthusiasm one may outstep the bounds of
propriety and so injure rather than benefit the cause. Total
Abstinence requires no explanation, the words carry an explanation with them. Temperance is more complicated, as
sometimes it borders on total abstinence. If I understand the
meaning given to it in our debate it means a moderate use of
intoxicating drinks. A temperance man is one who gives or
takes a dram. If cold he takes one to warm him, and if warm
to cool him; if sleepy it wakens him up, and sleepless it tran-
qualises his mind and sends him to the land of dreams: in a
word, it cures a' ills. Tippling would be a better term, however, we know what is meant.

Many have the idea that total abstinence is new, and must
be received with caution. That is not so. We hear of this and
that being "as old as the hills;" this I will not assert of T.A.,
but the phrase is often used of what is less true. The first
record we have of it dates back to about 1490 B.C., and it is
found in the 10th ch. of Leviticus ver. 9. "Do not drink wine
nor strong drink, thou, nor thy sons with thee, when ye go to
the tabernacle of the congregation, lest ye die. It shall be a
statue for ever throughout your generations".

.   .   .   .

Some think that by moderate drinking they are setting a

HIGH ST., TURRIFF. 14B066. G.W.W.

Turriff, where Robert Barclay worked as a tailor

Buckie, where Robert Barclay worked for Marquis Silverstine as a tailor

safer example, and showing more self-control than the opposite party. I beg to differ. Does it show more self-control to
partly than to wholly abstain? The abstainer sets the safest
example. Is there not in abstinence a grand opportunity for
the exercise of self-denial? Does not Paul inculcate this when
he says, "It is good neither to eat flesh nor to drink wine, nor
anything whereby thy brother stumbleth, or is offended, or is
made weak". He would have abstained even from eating flesh
for the sake of others, he says, "If meat make my brother
offend, I will eat no flesh while the world standeth, lest I
make my brother to offend". Many use drink who admit
they could do without it. They must drink for more grati-
fication, is that a safe example. If followed we know the result. Some who drink can remain sober for a time, but let
them taste — let the desire for strong drink be crossed, and
they will have it at all hazard. There are many such, what
advantage would moderate drinking be to them? In T.A.
there is help. Temperance as understood tonight cannot help
the drunkard, and put him in safety, keep drink away from
him and he is safe. (I am speaking from a moral standpoint).

Drinking in moderation cannot keep its votaries safe,
little by little they are sucked by the tide of intemperance
till, if not rescued they are seized by a demon who holds
them as captives. Take the case of the most confirmed drunkard, he never meant to become such. Once, perhaps, he advocated moderation, but slowly yet surely his temperance
gave way to intemperance and by and by he became a drunkard. In the days when he advocated temperance he had a wife
and children for whom he would have almost sacrificed his
all. Now and again he went home slightly the worse from
liquor. There was nothing very far wrong with him, he treated
his family lovingly as before, but, soon a difference was mani-
fest. The keen eye of the wife looked out into a future and
the thought forced itself upon her, "What if some day I become a drunkard's wife?" It could not be, her husband was
temperate. Days and months passed, the husband worked on,
but he had changed; for instead of spending his evenings at
home, he stayed out, often till midnight. He did not always
come home drunk, but his breath told a tale. Matters as yet
went on smoothly at his home, most of his wages he brought
home to the wife, upon whose cheeks the roses were still in
bloom, and a bright smile met him as he crossed his door
threshold while the merry laughter of the children fell as
sweet as rain upon his ears. But, by and by the rose faded on

that woman's cheek, and her brightly smiling countenance
assumed a care-worn aspect. The merry laughter of the children too, was not heard so often, as mother was ill and could
not bear it as in by-gone days. What caused this great change?
The husband and father came home often the worse of drink,
and at times when under its influence would bad use his wife
and children, his doings also caused hunger and want to be
felt in that home. Step by step that man sank till he lost his
situation, and left his family to be cared for by others. The
mother died, the children were scattered; the husband and
father where is he? "Ask of the winds if they can tell!" Perhaps in a drunken carousel he killed someone and was hanged,
or perhaps far, far from his once happy home he is found
dead, a paragraph states that the body of a man was found in
the ditch, at the roadside, who the night before was seen in
the vicinity much the worse of drink. He is buried in a
stranger's grave "Far far from home and kindred"; and the
curtain drops over the sad scene. This is no haphazard pic-
ture, but one by far too common, and will be until TOTAL
ABSTINENCE becomes more general. "Prevention is better
than cure" we are told.

.   .   .   .

There is a difference between TOTAL ABSTINENCE and
Drunkenness as there is a difference between the ocean and
the dry land. The moderate drinker leaves the dry land and
ventures into the great ocean of intemperance, and sees no
danger. If it does appear he will speedily come ashore. Far
out he knows are the raging billows of drunkenness, but he
never intends to encounter them, he only means to sport on
the water's edge. It is not necessary to go far from land to
lose one's life by drowning, many lose their lives in a few
inches of water, and folks are drowned while bathing, they
ventured too far and the result was, they perished. So with
moderate drinking: its votaries too often go beyond their
depth, by degrees they go out a little further, and sad to tell,
one day they cannot return. Safety lies in keeping as far from
the drink as possible; as one said, "If ye never drink, you'll
never get drunk".

.   .   .   .

T.A. is worthy of being upheld, not only from a Scriptural

and religious viewpoint but also from a humane and moral one.

"It forms a good foundation, against intoxication,
Or other degradation, or open violation
Which leads to ruination, which causes consternation,
At the final consummation.
It frees you from temptation, which would lead to ruination
With no chance of renovation. So under this persuasion
Hold no communication, with noxious emanation
Of brewer's fermentation, nor any vain libation
Producing stimulation.
To this determination, I call consideration
And without hesitation, I invite co-operation;
Not doubting invitation, will raise your estimation
And by continuation, afford you consolation;
For in participation, with this association,
You may by meditation insure the preservation
Of a future generation, from drunken exaltation
Which is a degradation to our own or any nation".

.   .   .   .

MEG MICHIE'S POT

A few hundred yards south of Balgaveny, in a hollow, between the lands of Glenythan and Hatton near the upper end
of a small valley forming part of the boundary between the
parishes of Auchterless and Forgue (but now included in
Ythanwells), may be seen three marshy bogs, in which are
some pools of stagnant water, usually termed "moss pots",
from which moss for fuel at one time had been taken. There
is little about these "pots" to arrest attention, unless, perhaps,
in Summer, when they, to a great extent, are overgrown by
wild flowers, the most notable of which is the buckbean, or
marsh trefoil (monyanthes trifoliata) one of the prettiest of
our native wild flowers. The visitor will be amply rewarded
by paying the place a visit when these flowers are in full
bloom, unless he be like Peter Bell, of whom the poet writes:

"A primrose by the river's brim
A simple primrose was to him,
And it was nothing more".

Peter Bell, seemingly, was dead to the beauties of nature. I
might mention that buckbean once had a place in the phar-
macopeia but is now discarded although used at times as a
medicine, and as a substitute for hops in the making of home-
made beer.

The nether marsh is at the lower end of a place called the
"Owl's Den", the north side of which was once adorned with
weed, but now cultivated, the south side, however, remains
waste. A hundred yards further up the valley is the second
marsh, the pond which is known as "Meg Michie's Pot".
Fifty yards further on is a third one but of it nothing interesting can be told; except that in it the wild flowers are
more abundant than in the other two.

"Meg Michie's Pot" owes its title to a personage of that
name who, about the close of the 18th century, drowned herself therein. It is a black, stagnant pool, six feet in diameter,
and 3 to 4 in depth, on one side of a nearly oval bog, 60 to
70 yards in circumference. (It is now overgrown with wild
flowers.)

In one of the humble abodes in Balgaveny hamlet, there
lived, long ago, two sisters named respectively Chirsty and
Margaret Michie, or "Meg" as she was usually termed. Of
Chirsty nothing worthy of narration had been handed down
by tradition. She seems to have been "like ither folk"; while
her sister was quite the opposite, being a half-daft and eccen-
tric sort of body, one that would be spoken of as having "a
bee in her bonnet", for in one of her "high gees" she made
an attempt to end her days by hanging herself in a barn near
her dwelling. It is not stated what prevented her from carrying
out this purpose fully, but some hitch evidently had occurred,
for Meg, while in a half-hanged condition, is said to have
taken a copper kettle containing money belonging to herself
and sister, and making all possible haste to the "pot" which
now bears her name, she threw it in and followed herself. Her
body was duly recovered, and buried at the upper end of the
"Owl's Den", the custom of the times forbidding that suicides
should be buried in a churchyard. A small boulder of "heathen
stone" is near the place of interment, although the exact spot
cannot now be pointed out, changes having been effected
both by time and the hand of man. For long this was looked
on as an "uncanny" place, more so after nightfall, it being
said that Meg at times might still be seen moving about. But
that has passed away, and the den may now be visited even at
midnight without the slightest fear crossing the mind.

"Up Aultdavie and down Owl's Den,
There Meg Michie sits pluckin' a hen".

So ran the once popular couplet but whether referring to her in the body or otherwise I cannot say. Enough for those of the olden times that, "O'er all there hung a shadow and a fear, A sense of mystery the spirit daunted, And said as plain as whisper in the ear, The place is haunted".

Meg's body, as already stated, was duly recovered and attended to, but all efforts to get hold of the kettle and its contents proved fruitless, either owing to the depth of water in the "pot" (at that time 16 to 20 feet) or from some mysterious cause which I cannot explain. The hole gradually got filled by being made a receptacle for stones and other debris, the writer along with many companions, now scattered or gone, having spent (perhaps I should say mis-spent) many an hour gathering material to put into it. "Happy time it was for all of us; but for me a time of rapture."

Robert Gordon, — see page 8 — had a firm belief that the kettle could be recovered and frequently visited the pot with an iron rod for the purpose of taking it out, but his utmost efforts, according to his own statement, only resulted in bringing the rod into contact with the "bow" of the kettle. But to return.

THE MYSTERIOUS WARNING

Early one morning, after Meg's funeral, 2 natives of Balgaveny went to the pot with pails etc., on purpose to lave it and secure the treasure at its bottom. All went well with them for a time, and there being no visible inlet for water, that element, after a deal of hard work was reduced, and the object of their search exposed to view — all now remaining to be done was to lay hold of it and draw it up; but alas! — "The best laid schemes o' mice an' men Gang oft a-gley".

The arrangements for its removal were almost complete, when a voice overhead suddenly cried out and alarmed them:-

"Bonnie Balgaveny's a' in a lowe,
Gine ye dinna believe me, rin up to the knowe".

Greatly alarmed, they left the hole, and running to the knowe
where a full view of Balgaveny was had, an act occupying
but a few seconds, they cast an eager look towards the hamlet but saw no sign of fire. Anxious to complete their work,
they returned to the hole; but only to meet with a fresh surprise, for to their dismay it had, during their short absence,
completely filled with water, thus placing the kettle and its
contents as far out of reach as ever. It need hardly be stated
that this singular occurrence prevented them from making
any further effort to secure the treasure, nor has any other
attempt been made since that time — "Stronie's" excepted.

BALGAVENY AND SURROUNDINGS

Balgaveny is no longer worthy the name of a hamlet. The
rows of ash and elm trees remain, giving to it when seen
from a distance a somewhat similar appearance as in by-gone
years, but a near view shows that a great change has taken
place. At one time there were thirty dwelling-houses in it,
now there is but one — a modern farmhouse with commodious
office houses. Two ruins remain, reminding us that there
once existed what was known as the "Toune o' Balgaveny".
A similar tale could be told of other of "Scotia's scattered
hamlets", which have passed from sight and are all but forgotten. Two roads intersect this place, one leading from the
Forgue and Aberdeen turnpike (a few hundred yards eastward) to Ythanwells, and the other leading towards Aucharnie from Hassiewells. The latter was once the highway to
Aberdeen before the turnpike was made, but by and by it
ceased to be used as a thoroughfare, most of it having been
ploughed up and added to the adjoining fields. Pinder, of
circus fame, took advantage of it and so shunned the tollbar
at Netherthird. A little above Balgaveny, a road branched off
passing through Balgaveny wood, (where faint traces of it can
still be seen,) through the Den of Largue, thence by Brae of
Largue, and on to Kirk of Forgue, etc. On the farm of Easter
Aucharnie, just where the road emerged from Balgaveny
wood, is a small knoll (not at all conspicuous) which was
pointed out to the writer as being the place where a cadger,
who had incurred the vengeance of the laird of Frendraught,
was hanged. The circumstances were said to be as follows —

He had asked his wife who she thought was the best looking man in the kirk of Forgue: unfortunately, her choice fell on the poor cadger, who accordingly was taken while vending his fish in this neighbourhood, and put to death, tradition says that his pony was allowed to wander about with the creels and their contents on its back until they rotted and fell off, no one daring to interfere. Those were the times when "lairds had power o' pot an' gallows". In the vicinity is a place called Gallowbog, a name indicating that at some period in the past there had been a place for execution at no great distance.

In the lower end of the Den of Largue, springing out of the rock and close to the road, is a small well, known as "the fairie's well"; the "fairy howe" being a little further on, but the luxuriant crop of wild rasperries is a greater source of attraction to visitors in Summer than both well and howe.

I quote the following from a local newspaper, written by the late Mr [James] Webster merchant, Balgaveny, who visited the district after an absence of several years.

.   .   .   .

Many years after the above appeared in the papers, the Free Church congregation (then the United Free) did bestir themselves and had the old building remodelled and greatly improved.

Half a mile east from Den of Largue is the hill of Denmoss, from which a good sight of the surrounding country may be had including a small portion of the Moray Firth near Macduff. On its eastern side, where the road from Gariochsford to Haremoss passes, is a large stone (conglomerate) called the "Wolf Stane". When or why it got this name I cannot say: probably it has been a landmark for centuries, several laird's lands meeting at it. In an old description of the Lands of Lessendrum mention is made of "Wolf Holes", which are supposed by some to have been holes dug to indicate the march, and so may have been this stone.

THE KIRKHILL, STONE CIRCLES, ETC.

The Kirkhill, half a mile south of Balgaveny, (mentioned on page 1) — somewhat conical in shape, is a hill from which an extensive view of the country far and near can be obtained. It is said that long ago, an attempt was made to erect a kirk upon it, but during the night, what had been built was knocked down and the stones scattered. From this it was concluded that the site was not the proper one so, in their extremity, they put a broom bush into the Ythan, which flows along its southern base, and nearby to where it stopped the kirk was to be built. It is said to have done so opposite to where the parish church of Auchterless now stands, which may account for its being a little towards the lower end of the parish. On the north side of the hill is a hollow said to have been used by the Comyns as a war trench, but beyond local tradition, I have come across nothing to confirm this. I remember, however, having seen pits between the trench and the hill top which were supposed to have been used by the sentinels placed a short distance apart and who, by this means, kept open a line of communication between the hill top and the camp below and reported the enemy movements.

On the west side of the hill is a gully through which the burn of Aultdavie runs. In an edition of "Pratt's Buchan" I read some years ago, it was stated that this was the Ythan's first tributary, entering it a half mile below its source. This is not so. It is two miles fully, and two streamlets join it further up, one at Meadowhead and one at Glenmailen, near the northwest corner of the Roman camp on the farm of Buss. Had the railway passed through Forgue instead of going to Gartly, it would have gone up what I have termed a gully, and entered it at the "Cadger Howe". I quote from a booklet written by Mr Matheson, Forgue's first Free Church minister. He writes as follows:-

> "When the Great North of Scotland Railway was projected, the first intention was to take it through Forgue, passing close to the Free Church. The survey was made, and but for the opposition of some landlords, who foolishly wished to keep a railway at a distance from their properties, and the astuteness of one who, by offering land on the easiest terms, induced the railway company to take the line round by Kennethmont, the Great North line would have opened up the kingdom of Forgue, and brought it into immediate communication with all the rest of the country. Who can say what changes the railway might have brought into this quiet, secluded district?"

On the east side of the hill, on Logie-Newton farm, are

Banff

BROAD ST. PETERHEAD, LOOKING EAST. 201. G.W.W.

Peterhead

three stone circles (probably Druidical, although differing considerably from those in other places). The stones, not large, are mostly quartz, and seemingly, have been brought from a distance. (See Mr Gurnell's book, Standing Stones, etc., Huntly Field Club.) In an adjoining field to the south of the circles is a single standing stone, conoidal in form 2 x 3 x 5 girth at the thickest part 8 feet. There are other circles in the parish, but some of them have been utilised for building purposes and the site ploughed up. The following was related to me some years ago:- A new tenant had leased a farm where new houses had to be put up, on this there was a circle, and it was blasted and built into the steading. In course of time sickness broke out among the cattle, and it was suggested that this was caused by the breaking up of the stones of the circle, and it was also suggested that they might look for any of the stones and put them back to the site; this was done, and a chip of a stone found its way back to its old place. I forget if I heard how it fared with the cattle afterwards. Sometime previous to my hearing this related I had occasion to pass the site, and found a chip of a stone, which was in keeping with what I was told was put back. I took it home with me; perhaps I erred.

THE ROMAN CAMP AT GLENMELLAN

South of the Kirkhill, across the Ythan, and a mile from its source, is the ROMAN CAMP, sometimes called the Re-Hill and Re-dykes — considerable portions of the dyke which formed part of the camp's defence still remain: but there is little now to arrest attention, and where the Roman soldiers ages ago encamped we now find well cultivated fields with horses, cattle and sheep peacefully grazing thereon.

.   .   .   .

A few words as to the probable origin of the name Glenmellan which I suppose comes from the Gaelic gleann a glen, and meallan a little lump or hump, or perhaps mulian a little hillock or bluff, hence Glenmellan — the glen with the little hump or hillock. Let one stand on the south side of the glen, a little above the farm steading and looking towards what is

known as the "Bunon Hillock", they will then see the appro-
priateness of the name, which is fairly descriptive of the place,
as all place-names of Gaelic origin are. Of this place I say in
the words of the poet. -

> "Fair scenes for childhood's opening bloom,
> For sportive youth to stray in".

[ROBERT HALL'S DIARY]

The following is from a diary kept by a Mr Robert Hall,
blacksmith and farmer at Bilbo, Auchterless, and embraces a
period from 1789 to 1833, in which year Mr Hall died in his
80th year. It is mostly of a religious nature, giving the text as
also notes of sermons and lectures he had listened to during
those years, but in addition to this is much interesting matter
giving us a glimpse of the district and times a hundred years
ago. I am indebted to Mr James Alexander, Ythanwells, for
giving me the diary which is now in a dilapidated state, many
leaves being lost. A Mr Rose was minister at Auchterless,
previous to December 1810 when he died, and was succeeded
by Mr Dingwall in September 1811 who was minister for 50
years. Mr Rose had been minister for 36 years.

On July 23rd 1803 the foundation stone of the Kirk at
Bogfountain was laid by Alexander Christie, mason, Upper
Lenshie, in the presence of John, Robert and Patrick Hall.
And some days later they brought wood from Pitmachie, and
stones from Bennachie for it. The length is about 41 feet long
by 54 wide over walls. No mention is made of the opening of
it, but I find a service was held in it on January 22nd 1804,
by a Mr Paterson. A Mr Walter Graham was minister and
schoolmaster for many years — first mentioned May 1805,
and the last reference to him is in December 1820. Mr Hall's
last mention of Bogfountain is in May 1828, when a Mr Robb
from Tough preached. The kirk has been for long used as a
dwelling-house, and the manse, on the other side of the road
and latterly the dwelling-house on a small farm, has disappeared; and the fields, like many around it added to adjoining
farms.

A school was built a little to the east, in 1815, messrs.
Hall driving wood for it from Hatton. Isabella Mearns was

teacher there for long. It was used till about 1880, but has now vanished. Previous to the building of the kirk, meetings were held at Graystone. On 8th February 1813 is the following:- "Died here on Friday last Margaret Fraser, a cripple woman, who has been carried on a barrow for many years, and is said to have been the wife of one W. Young, a tinker or country brazler, to whom she bare 18 sons. She had lost in a great measure the use of speech as well as the use of her limbs by a shock of blasting long ago, so that she could not be rightly understood, but she appeared to retain her intellectual faculties to the last, and even spoke so as to be partly understood a few hours before she breathed her last. She came or rather I should say, was brought in a cart from Headtown, Knockleith on Friday the 29th ult. and died that day week about 12 o'clock noon. During that time she frequently expressed her gratitude for the kind offices done to her in the most affectionate manner. She had 3 shillings and 3 pence halfpenny sterling in copper and a counterfeit shilling. John Wood got three shillings sterling for making her coffin. Alexander Robb, farmer in Newton furnished most of the wood gratis, to whom we are much indebted for his judicial and friendly advice and other assistance on the occasion. I paid 5/8 sterling out of my own property to John Shivis, for muslin and nails, and a shilling to James Forbes kirk-officer, for digging her grave; besides all other necessary expenses and trouble to the family that behoved necessarily to attend the circumstances on such an occasion. A piece of blanket, together with her other rags, was given to James Sandieson, a poor man, a native of, and residing in the parish". Where was Headtown, also Knowehead? both named as near Knockleith. Blotted out, eh?

Frequent mention is made of a George Manson in Demerara with whom he corresponded; he was his brother-in-law, and once sent home £100 to Mrs Hall, his sister as a present. This is the only time I find any reference made to his wife.

George Manson, Demerara! This recalls the days of my childhood. Ever since I remember George, who was known by the sobriquet of "Demerara". was in the farm of Middle Hassiewells, opposite my father's croft, leaving about the time I went to school. He was succeeded by George Taylor, who died in a short time, but his family kept the holding till Whitsunday 1899, when they rouped out and went to Aberdeen for a time (I was clerk at the roup). After staying in the city for a short period they removed to the farm of Hillhead,

Lightnot, near Oldmeldrum, where George and Bella all now alive still are, while I write these notes in September 1923. The family consisted of Mrs Taylor, two sons, and two daughters. Of all I must write in the most complimentary terms, Mrs Taylor was a woman above the average for intelligence, and very kindhearted. She died on 26th of April, 1906. James who was of a most cheerful, and agreeable disposition, while yet in his prime he became the victim of a form of gout which laid him aside from work for many years during which he suffered much. He died 11th May 1910. Maggie qualified as a nurse, and filled various situations in the capacity satisfactorily. She retired some years previous to her death which took place at Lightnot on 18th September 1920. All three are buried at Oldmeldrum.

.   .   .   .

I return to Mr Hall. The weather was not always the best for harvest work in his time any more than now, as the following entries show:- "1812 Began on Tuesday the 22nd of September to cut down our barley, by 11th October it was mostly got in and the oat harvest begun. The crop in this neighbourhood is great, but the generality of it is yet very green. The Summer till about Lammas was generally rainy, but for some time past has been very agreeable, unless some frost at night which is said to have done hurt in some places. 12th October: Rain and fog. 4th November: Finished cutting the corn; the harvest has been rainy and by reason of the lateness of the season and early frosts there will be a failure of grain, but the fodder plenty. Within these few days the weather has been dry and a great deal of the crop got in, in tolerably good condition. In this district some have in all the crop, others a good deal of it still exposed. 20th November: This day we took in the remainder of our corn, but there is still a great quantity in the neighbourhood still exposed, and the farther up the country still the more. The earth is covered with frost and snow, the present dispensation of Providence is very threatening, but yet there is much mercy in it, for in this part of the country there is already more of the crop saved than could have been expected in the beginning of, and during the harvest. Glory be to Thy Name Gracious God, the wise disposer of all events, and Bountiful giver of all good. The weather since the 20th November has been frosty, with snow, (but moderate) unless some green days now and then.

The crop is now got in, in our neighbourhood, but is much damaged in several places, before it was cut, and in the stook, and in the yard. The crop in general is very deficient, but although it is deficient, yet it is very wholesome. Blessed be God".

I quote from the following year:- 1813. 10th April: "The storm that came on on the 1st instant went off in about a week, although it was said to be the greatest fall of snow in such a short time now remembered. 12th: Began to sow here, the weather continues fine. We also sowed our lint, and planted early potatoes. 8th September: Began to cut down our bere, and the oats on the 21st. The weather through the latter part of the Summer and what is past of the harvest has been uncommonly fine. 4th October: This day was rainy. James Wilson, Loop of Towie, brought us home an 8 day clock, which he has made for us, the price is £7.10. 21st: We took in the remainder of our corn. 29th: The harvest in this neighbourhood is now concluded, the weather all through this month has been very variable, and sometimes great falls of rain by which the crop is partly damaged. But notwithstanding there is abundance for man and beast. It has been very hard on the poor for a 12 month past, vitals being high and manufactories low".

Again he writes: "The crop last year being short, fodder has been very scarce, and if the weather continues bad but a very short time, it is to be feared that several people's cattle will starve: if it had not been for the good of the whin bush, the country had been in a much worse case than it is".

I pick out a few lines embracing incidents extending over many years. Of the stone — a table one, about 6 by 3 feet, that marks their resting place in Auchterless kirkyard he writes: "The stone cost £2 at Auchendore, from which place my brothers, John, Patrick, James and I brought it here, undressed. Adam Maitland from Drumblade dressed, lettered, and painted it, in about three weeks, which cost us about two guineas, besides his board during that time: my 3 brothers and I defrayed the expenses".

Mention is made of many stormy and tempestuous days, doing a deal of damage both by sea and land — uncommon storms of thunder and lightning, in one instance a woman being killed at Drumblair, Forgue, during a thunderstorm. Often the Sundays were of so tempestuous a nature as to put church-going out of the question. Then there were severe winters, with snow and frost that continued for a long time,

and stopping water mills for weeks on end; also heavy rains
that did harm to the crops. On 4th October 1807 a comet
appeared in the west, and in December 1811 he says "There
has a comet appeared for some months, but has now almost
disappeared. Some say it has been the occasion of the great
heat we have experienced during the time of its nearness to
us".

On 13th August 1816 "There was an earthquake generally
felt throughout Scotland about 11 o'clock at night". I have
heard my mother speak of an earthquake occurring when she
was very young: being born in June 1812 she would have
been 4 years old, so this is likely the same one. Many markets
at which he bought and sold are now extinct; among others I
might mention Hawkhall, Slioch, and Wartle. Huntly and
Turriff have Auction Marts now.

On 6th August 1803 he attended a meeting held in the
parish Church, Auchterless, to consider what could be done
for defending the country in case of invasion by the French;
and here he enrolled as a volunteer for defence of the realm.
On 12th June 1810, he was married to Isabella Manson, by
Mr Rose, Auchterless.

"Bilbo, 26th April, 1820. Died here James Chalmers, at 2
o'clock this morning of only 24 hours illness: the fatal com-
plaint was inflammation of the bowels. A serious warning to
every individual in this family, and others to be in readiness
for our departure out of time". Again he writes:- "3rd August 1821. Garden Duff Esq., of Hatton, and Mr William
Cowie were here inspecting the marches or landmarks". 29th
August. "This day Messrs Garden Duff of Hatton and George
Leslie, Badenscoth, were here settling the marches between
Logie Newton and Bibo, etc.; and appointed 3 stones to be
placed, 1 below the road, 1 in the bog at the hard hillock,
and 1 at the march of Littlemill, and a ditch to be cast 4 feet
wide".

A TRIBUTE TO THE LATE ROBERT HALL, BILBO

Someone added the following tribute to his memory after
having looked over the portion of the diary devoted to religious matters:- He says, "From a review of the foregoing
precious portions of sacred Scripture so carefully recorded,

much salutary instruction may be derived. How many re-
flections may naturally arise in our minds on the many and
distinguishing privileges which we have enjoyed by the light
of the Gospel among us. How great our responsibility! How
great our happiness if suitably improved! How inexcusable if
we neglect so great salvation!

The pious, steady and persevering spirit of our dead
friend may at once be perceived by the foregoing manuscript,
which comprehends a period of upward of 43 years and it is
to be hoped the plan might be adopted, and improved by
some pious person into whose hands it may fall.

It is not here intended to attempt to delineate the character of him whom we firmly trust his Lord and Master has
already honoured with the appellation of 'Good and faithful
servant'. All that is meant, is only to make a few plain remarks, to the truth of which, we trust none will object. It
will readily be allowed by all who had any intimate acquaintance with him, that he was of a truly devout and upright disposition, that the many prevailing vices and immoralities of
this corrupt and degenerate age, appeared to be matter of real
sorrow and grief to him, and on the contrary any accounts of
the succcess or revival of religion, either at home or abroad,
gave him the greatest of delight. His natural endowments
were of the ordinary class, and his education such as the circumstances of his parents could afford, but much improved
by unremitting diligence. But it becomes us to say with the
apostle: that it was 'by the grace of God that he was what he
was'.

Though it pleased a Wise Providence to place him in a
humble and obscure station he was nevertheless of a public
spirit, and to hear of the prosperity of religious institutions in
particular, afforded him real pleasure, such as Bible, missionary, and Sabbath school societies, anything in short that
tended to promote the glory of God, and the advancement of
the Redeemer's kingdom in the world: and though unable to
do much by pecuniary means for their support, they had his
constant and fervent prayers.

The best interests of the rising generation occupied a
chief room in his affections, and in 1819 he joined with several
other Christian friends in instituting a Sabbath evening school,
and in forming a society for its support, of which society he
was chosen president, which office he held till the day of his
death. The school was attended by the children in the neighbourhood, and met with every expected success, under the

tuition of him and Peter Calder, the latter of whom in 1831 removing to Aberdeen, the sole charge of the school developed on our departed friend. It is also well known, that he had a very active hand in establishing the subscription school at Ladybog, in procuring subscribers, and by personal appli- cation (in name of the society) to Mr Duff of Hatton, obtained a grant of a spot of land for a school and garden, on the land of Ladybog. In short the school was erected and everything put in fair train, and though the encouragement for a school- master was very limited (being only a free house and garden and school fees) yet the school has been supplied with able and successful teachers, and many are reaping the benefit of the institution. But as many of the members of the society have since its commencement been removed, some by death and others by distance of place, and few new members join- ing, the number is greatly reduced and our friend, who had been their president for 16 years, in returning home from a quarterly meeting (for the last time) on Thursday 7th March 1833 was seized with severe illness (supposed a stroke of apoplexy) which on the morning of Sabbath 17th March ter- minated his earthly labours.

It may be truly said he was a lover of mankind, a friend to the poor, as far as his circumstances would permit, a ready visitor of the sick throughout his neighbourhood, a careful observer of the conduct of Divine Providence especially with respect to himself, family and friends, as appears by some notes taken down by him on that and other subjects. But though much taken up with spiritual matters, his secular affairs were not neglected, and regular account taken of work done, both in the field and garden throughout the year, with remarks on the weather and the seasons, and all his other accounts and matters of any moment, left in a correct and regular state. — But to say no more, as a man and a Christian he studied to have a life and conversation becoming the Gos- pel. Let us all go and do likewise. 'Blessed are they that do God's commandments, that they may have a right to the tree of life, and enter in through the gates into the city'. — 'The memory of the just is blessed. The righteous shall be had in everlasting remembrance'. Amen". Perhaps this was never printed before!

.   .   .   .

FROM SERVANT TO MASTER

I left Gordonstown at Whitsunday, 1877 and began tailoring on my own account at Glenythan, Ythanwells, as also doing other odd jobs, including harvest work, to make ends meet. Here we had some rather severe snowstorms, including the notable one of 1881, when our humble abode was all but put out of sight by the great accumulation of snow, the result of 3 days continuous drifting. In the kitchen a lamp had to be kept lighted for 2 days on end, it being in total darkness; the other end had some light. When the drifting abated we had to take the snow from off the roof, the wreath being as high as the chimney. There was a belt at the back of the house, and it caused the snow to accumulate on our front, so that when the thaw came we had more water about us than we cared for; for a strong spring bubbled up at the fireside, and ran out at the door for about a week. But although we had big storms in after years, we never had a similar experience. I put a drain round the house; perhaps it may have done good.

It was at this stage of life that I was associated with a Mutual Improvement Class at Ythanwell, and this was how the articles on Temperance and the Shetland Trip came to be written. Many of the members were old school-mates, and some belonged to an older and some to a younger school. Among those who are dead I might name George Skinner, senior, Sunnyside, one who, although getting over in years took a deep interest in the class and, set a good example to the younger members. Then there was James Forbes, Glenythan, John Macpherson, Dryburn; Peter Simpson, Glencoe; G. Stephen, Glenmailen; Robert Troup, Ythanwells, and others at present forgotten. A few abide where they were over 40 years ago; viz. — James Alexander, Ythanwells; William Alexander, Monellie; and John Tierney, Drumdolla. William Kidd, then living at Drumdolla, after being a number of years in Glenfoudland, has settled down at Denhead, Glenythan; near to where Andrew Garden lived who, after a few years stay at Littlefollo, has made his home at Cairnhill, on the lythe [sheltered] side of the hill of Culsalmond. James M'Hattie tenants a small farm at Brae of Largue. James Tocher, Lochmoss, is now at Rothienorman. Isaac Troup, born and living at East Cranloch up to Whitsunday, 1923, now lives on the "Kingdom of Forgue". near to the historic "Howe of Frendraught". His brother James, after being many

years in America, returned, married, and lives in Glenfound-
land. Alexander J.M. Troup, who was secretary to the class,
removed from the Bisset Banks to Insch. F. Stephen is at
Suttie, near Kintore. Others I might name have gone further
afield and of their present whereabouts I can say nothing. As
for myself I have gone "down the water", as mentioned by
my companion James Duguid (see page 18), and live near the
old castle of Towie-Barclay, of which I quote the following
description, as given in the BANFFSHIRE JOURNAL for
March, 1887:- "Over the principal entrance is this inscription,
'Sir Alexander Barclay of Tolly, foundator. decessit A.D.
1136' and on the same stone is carved, 'In time of valth all
men sims frendly: a frind is not knowing but in adversitie
1593'. This fine old place is said to have remained pretty
entire till 1792, when, to suit the ideas of an unromantic
occupying tenant, rude hands were laid upon it. The roof,
turrets, and embrasures were removed, the height reduced to
two stories, and on it placed a common roof. At the suggestion
of an occupier of different taste, the proprietors had this removed in 1887, and, for its better protection, and to be made
more in harmony with its original form, an embattled parapet
has been put on, with flat-headed turrets at the four corners.
and cement roof. Inside the old baronial hall the arched roof
is very fine. A house in keeping with the place has been greatly
beautified by the present occupier". Mr Scott, United Free
Church, Auchterless, preaches in the Hall on the 2nd, 4th,
and 5th Sundays of the month, at 5 o'clock P.M.; and the
Episcopalian Church minister Fyvie, on the 1st Sunday during
the Summer months.

MUTUAL IMPROVEMENT SOCIETIES

Before I was out of my teens I was a member of a society
that met in the Free Church Forgue, and latterly in the class-
room after it was built. For a while I was a listener, doing or
saying nothing, but by and by I took part in what was being
discussed etc. Once I was put down for the negative side of a
debate on a subject I knew nothing about, viz. "Can Scotland
Complain of Injustice fron England?" I objected taking it on,
but was put down for it in spite of all protests. A friend came
to the rescue saying that he would help me; as the time went

past, I reminded him of his promise, and this is what he said:-
"You stand up and say, Mr Chairman and Gentlemen, you all
know the subject for debate tonight, viz. 'Can Scotland Complain of Injustice from England?' I emphatically say that such
is not the case, and with those words I sit down". This was all
the help I got, so the sequel was that I absented myself from
the meeting and the late Mr Keys, then schoolmaster at
Gariochsford, filled the vacant place. Sometime later, however, I managed to take a leading side in a debate but without
compulsion. I was a member of another class held one Winter
at Gariochsford but it did not long survive. The one at the
Free Church continued for many years: the one at Ythanwells
for 2 or 3 sessions. The Gariochsford class was what might be
named a reading club, members gave readings which were
criticised, etc.

In the Spring of 1885 we went to the upper flat of the
Old School, then vacant, at Gariochsford. While here I was 4
or 5 harvests at Upper Leashie with Mr James Lumsden. The
3 harvests, 1883 to 1885 I was at Goukswell, Culsalmond,
with the late Mr Alexander Weir. Other harvests were taken
doing day's work at several places, sometimes only making
out a week in the course of 2 or 3 according to the state of
the weather, etc.

In August 1894, I was appointed to do a short postal
walk from Thorniebank via Gariochsford, Balgaveny shop
etc. and back to starting point with collection to William
Swanson, postman from Turriff. This took about an hour
daily, the pay being 2/6 weekly but, as I lived at the wrong
end of the walk, I had four miles to do daily, for which I had
no remuneration. I began 27th August, 1894, and retired
after putting in 27 years, on 31st August 1921.

After a time the pay was increased to 3/- weekly, and the
collecting as far as possible done on the outward journey;
anything I got when delivering was handed to the Forgue
postman. This meant a little more pay and less travelling.
When the house-to-house delivery began in December 1898
my walk was extended, I became a Rural Auxiliary Postman,
got uniform, and the wages raised to 7/6, and in a short time
to 8/- when Gallowbog and Hillhead of Aucharnie were put
on to my walk. This continued up till September 1912, when
I was transferred to a walk from Auchterless Station as the
one I had been so long on was to be incorporated with one
from Rothienorman. After 1898 the Gariochsford district
was served from Auchterless instead of Turriff as formerly:

Alexander Brown, Kirkton, being postman, retiring in 1912. My new walk took me past Camalyns, Steinmanhill, Lendrum, the Brownhills, Backmill, Lescraigie, Broadford, Woodend, Greenbrae, Loop, and several other places not mentioned. This walk was longer, and the wages rose to 10/6, and the holidays became 16 instead of 4.

In 1885 the lower flat of the Old School was occupied by John Morrison, whose wife, Jane Simpson, died there 21st April 1887, aged 73 years. Next year John removed to the Oldyoach, dying there in 1st December 1888, aged 74 years. Both are interred at Auchterless. The next Old School tenant was Alexander Stewart and his wife Margaret Clark who, after staying a few years, went to the North Lodge at Hatton Castle, to which a croft was attached. Sandie died in December 1906 and his widow left, finally settling down with a friend at Gordonstone, where she died; both are buried in the New Cemetery at Turriff. When they left the Old School I became tenant and continued so till September 1912, when, in order to follow my calling, I removed to Sillerton Cottage, Auchterless.

During my stay at the Old School I saw many changes — many ups and downs — heavy snowstorms, snow in June, thunder and lightning in harvest, blocked roads, retarding traffic and making walking a rather tiresome matter. The first Winter I posted we had a very heavy and prolonged snowstorm: W. Swanson had to discard his vehicle and do the round on horseback for a while, owing to the blocked state of the roads. The time of the Elliot disaster was a time to be remembered. George Clark, who was postman in Oldyoach and Pitglassie district (served from Thorniebank), like myself lived far from the railway, and so we did not know when to expect mails, but we always put in an appearance and at times got a vain travel, but I frequently went on to the Kirkton office with our collection. The forenoon of the Elliot disaster day I was in doubt as to what I should do and went part of my walk to see what folks would say I should do; I had not, however, gone very far when I had a good few parcels of a perishable nature to take with me if I did go, so this seemed to settle the matter, and away I went, but Sandie Brown did not appear. A man from Glenythan who had been looking for the Rothienorman post, to get a letter that had to be in Turriff by a certain time, came on the scene, who handed this missive to me. So after waiting for some time I left, hopeful of getting rid of my collection ere I had gone very far. The snow was deep; and to avoid missing A.B. I went past Knockleith House, having by this deeper snow to contend with than if I had kept the road. I had to go to the Kirkton office, so after food and rest I started for home, a friend going with me to Knockleith: who afterwards told me how trying he felt the return journey was to him. I got on all right, but progress was slow, and when within a half-mile from home I nearly succumbed to the fury of the tempest, but struggled on and got home in safety. At the end of the road leading from Ythanwells I met William Loban, carter, Balgaveny, who had to leave his horse and cart at Ythanwells and walk home; he, though a strong man in the prime of life, said that he had had enough of it, being nearly done up by the walk from that stormy district. In subsequent years storms have been fewer and less severe, the winters being milder, and the summers colder and less congenial.

Owing to infectious diseases and deaths in our house I was off duty on 3 different occasions, but, during those 27 years I was never once off work from personal sickness. I paid the National Insurance contributions from its commencement till I was 70, but never required doctor or drugs, perhaps chilblains was my worst ailment; but for this I was my own medical adviser. I also for a short time paid the Unemployment contributions, which does not merit my full approval like the National Health Insurance Act. I sympathise with those out of work, more so those with families, but young, strong, able-bodied fellows ought to have provision made for the proverbial "rainy day", and so be independent of the dole.

In the parish of Forgue there is an old ruin known as

THE OLD CASTLE OF BOGNIE

.   .   .   .

I have heard that it was built to give employment to people at a time when work was scarce. Perhaps this accounts for its not having been finished. The wages would likely have been small, and work reviving, the workmen may have asked for bigger pay, which being refused, brought the building to a standstill; and so this and other complications may be why it was never finished. Be that as it may, I see no reason why the work should not again be resumed, more so, in these times when there is so much unemployment to contend with all around. A short time ago I was in Huntly, and had a walk around the Old Castle, and saw that it was being put in a better condition so as to prevent it from becoming a complete ruin. The foundations of one older were also dug round and exposed. I believe the Government is doing this, and it will take a considerable time ere the work is finished, and will mean the expenditure of a pretty round sum of money; giving work to a good few in these times of unemployment; but, when the work is well accomplished, we will still have only a magnificent ruin to look at. Now were my suggestion carried out and the old castle of Bognie made into a home for disabled soldiers or others who, having served their day and generation, are no longer able to engage in life's active duties, to such this would be a welcome harbour of refuge; and the end accomplished would justify the outlay of making an old ruin into a magnificent abode.

On page 31 I mentioned that I had written to a local newspaper as to the state of Colonel Shand's monument on the Hawkhill, Forgue; and, how, afterwards the improvements I suggested were carried out. I would be pleased should a similar thing happen at the old castle at Bognie. Then there is Haddo House, Inverkeithnie, which for long has stood vacant, and fast becoming a ruin. Might not "the powers that be" step in and save it? Thus in some measure solving the house-less problem.

[AN UNFINISHED HOUSE]

There is an unfinished house at Carnoussie on the north bank of the Deveron, a few miles west from Turriff. This house was designed by Archibald Simpson, a notable Aberdeen architect, who did more than any single person who ever lived to give character and beauty to Aberdeen: his grave is in St Nicholas churchyard. The proprietor was a Captain Grant who committed suicide in 1841, while the mansion was being built. The roof was on, the first coat of plaster applied, but the flooring was not laid, and in this state it remains. The new proprietors of the estate, Harvey, never completed it, and there it stands desolate and empty, save for the use to which the farm manager puts some of its apartments as a joiner's workshop and storehouse.

. . . .

THE OLD CASTLE OF THE BOYNE NEAR PORTSOY

Hugh Miller in his "Rambles of a Geologist", and who passed through this district in 1847, mentions this ruin in the following terms:-

. . . .

A large portion of this ruin fell on the 10th February 1888. The Old Castle of Findlater, a miniature Gibraltar, and the principal residence of the Findlater family till the close of the 16th century, is a few miles to the west, in the parish of Fordyce. The Tower of Deskford, a short distance inland, belonged to the same family. It was demolished about 1840; it stood near to the old church. It was a lofty building of no great extent, with turrets and crow-stepped gables; and from its situation and surroundings could not have failed to be an attractive rural residence.

> "Oh! earthly grandeur! pompous glare of state;
> Where art thou fled? where's now thy splendid show?"

THE OLD CASTLE OF LESLIE, ABERDEENSHIRE

This ruin stands in the parish of Leslie, four miles south of Insch. It was founded June 17th 1661 by William Forbes of Leslie, who died in 1670 and was buried in the neighbouring churchyard. The building was adorned by five turrets, and enclosed within a rampart and moat with a drawbridge on the west guarded by a strong watch-tower, which had closed by a gate and portcullis. On the castle is the date 1664 which most likely is the year it was finished. On the south west of the castle is a place called Chapelton, where had been formerly a Roman Catholic Chapel, and near this, on the verge of the road leading to Alford, is a circular hollow called "The Four Lord's Seat", or 'Little John's Length", five feet in diameter and nearly four feet deep, where four Lords are said to have sat and dined on their own lands.

The castle of Licklyhead, the ancient seat of the Leith family, 2 or 3 miles to the east, was erected in 1663 by William Forbes of Leslie, and is still inhabited.

THE OLD CASTLE OF DUNIDEER, INSCH

A corruption of Dun-Do-Adhra (Gaelic), Mountain for the worship of God. The hill is nearly 3000 yards in circumference at the base occupying nearly 27000 square feet. On the summit of the hill, which rises to an elevation of 300 feet from the level plains of the Garioch, is a plain, and on the top there stands the vestige of a vitrified fortification or castle, having a chapel within its own walls, dedicated to St John. This castle is said to have been reared by Gregory the Great in A.D. 890, and was a seat of David, Earl of Huntington and Garioch in 1178, who also is said to have erected it; which last appears to be more authentic. The castle was surrounded by a strong rampart and fosse, the ruins of which are conspicuous. Without the ruins can be traced the remnants of many other buildings.

AUCHTERLESS AND FORGUE

I can write of no ruins "old and hoary" in Auchterless like the above: if such existed they have long since disappeared. The few most conspicuous ruins, perhaps, are a mealmill at Littlemill and one at Badenscoth, burned down some years ago. A sad tragedy took place here some years previous: a miller falling through the kiln, and narrowly escaped falling into the furnace. He, however, held on to the iron bars on which the plates rest, but was so badly burned that lock-jaw supervened, and he died soon after.

The condition of the kilns in country mills was looked into after this, and where needed put right. At Newmill is the ruin of a thrashing mill destoyed by fire many years ago, and never renewed.

A little further down we find a preserved ruin: viz. the bell gable and other portions of the walls of the old kirk, replaced by a new one built about 1877, with a spire added in 1896, and a clock placed on it in 1903. The date 1780 appears on the old gable. Still down the Ythan and we have a small bit of a ruin, part of a chapel that once was here (hence the name). St Mary's well is nearby, but the history of this place I fear is lost. What for long has been a vegetable garden is said to have been the burial ground attached to the chapel. A portion of it has been leveled to permit of its being used as a place of recreation, when relaxation is needed amidst life's sterner duties. At Chapelton, Drumblade, there is another disused graveyard, surrounded by a stone fence and having a holy well in the vicinity, but all trace of the chapel has vanished. The ground has been planted with trees which, over 30 years ago when I passed it, were about full grown and were being cut down. Perhaps a coming generation may plough it up. I heard that many years ago someone was to be buried here, and a part of the ground was gone over in search for a table stone supposed to have been covered by the soil, but it could not be found. I did not hear where the deceased was buried. The stone could ill have been found having been removed to the farm house for a door lintel. The farmer could have shown them the stone.

Dr Temple in his book on the Formartin district Aberdeenshire, mentions an old burial ground through which a march passed, and how the farmer on one side of it carted away the portion of it that lay next him to top-dress his fields. In a booklet published by the Established Presbytery of Turriff there is mention made of a recently discovered graveyard at Mains of Tollo, Inverkeithnie, but this is all the information given; possibly it is incorporated in a field on that farm. At Christ's Kirk near Insch, if I mistake not, there is another ancient burying place for long included in the bounds of the farm stackyard. All this treatment of old burial places I heartily disapprove of and condemn. The places have been set aside sometime in the distant past for the disposal of the dead, why not treat it as sacred ground and leave it alone "sacred to the memory of" those who in the years long gone past helped to make our country what it is today, and leave undisturbed the place where "The rude forefathers of the hamlet sleep"?

.   .   .   .

These lines [two poems on kirkyards and burials] written by some, to me, unknown poet, seem to fit in with the above remarks on kirkyards; now for a suggestion to those in authority. Why should they not take over these old burial-grounds, see that they were properly fenced and laid out for the reception of the dead — "a place to bury strangers in". This would provide some work for the unemployed as well.

MANSION HOUSES, PICT'S HOUSES, AND STONE CIRCLES

There are a few mansion houses in Auchterless, the only one I have never seen being the one at Blackford. Those at Badenscoth and Hatton Manor have long been occupied as farm houses. There is a more modern house at Knockleith, built about the middle of the 19th century and occupied for many years by the late Colonel Duff and family. Owing to the war it was used as a private boarding school, but after the Lady Principal was killed by falling off her bicycle in 1921 it ceased to be used as such.

On Mains of Hatton there is a stone circle, and a mile west on Pitglassie is another, one of the stones being cup-marked; but a farmer who wanted more ground, many years ago, huddled them all together. The cup-marks are on a stone 3 feet 6 inches high, with a crack in it; there are 8 marks, but they are rather indistinct. To the south on several fields the foundations of Pict's houses may be seen. This takes us back to days of long, long ago.

I now turn to Forgue. There are remnants of a stone circle at Wardend, and I think at Cairnton near Cobairdy; also in a wood at Hillhead of Frendraught. There may have been one near Balgaveny, as many stones similar to those in other circles have been broken up and built into the houses etc. Where the farmhouse of South Mains was, there is a stone which for long I have thought to be cup marked; also a smaller one built into a dyke at the new steading nearer the turnpike.

I tried to induce two antiquarian gentlemen to take a look at them and decide, but perhaps the game was not thought worth the candle, and the mystery is still unsolved. There was at one time a castle at Drumdollo, but all I saw of it some years ago, was a heap of stones near the farm house at Mains of Drumdollo. The mansion houses in Forgue would compare favourably with those in Auchterless; perhaps the most interesting one would be

FRENDRAUGHT HOUSE

of which I quote the following regarding it from the late Dr Temple, he says:- " 'Tristis et infelix semper inhospita turris'. 'O sad and unhappy and ever inhospitable tower' ".

So wrote Dr Arthur Johnston, the famous Latin poet of Caskieben. For many a long year this place was "sombre and solitary", but of late the gloom has been dispelled and it now wears a brighter aspect. The earliest account of it dates back to 1203, when Michael de Ferendrach appears as a witness to a charter given by William the Lyon. It would appear that Frendraught and Forgue were spoken of as separate parishes as late as 1699. For long it was the chief residence of the Crichtons of Crichton and Frendraught. In 1630 a sad calamity took place here known as the "burning of Frendraught" and celebrated in song, a long ballad being written on the event. A number of persons were on a visit to Sir James Crichton and his lady (the proprietors). After being well entertained all went to bed, the visitor's bedrooms being in the old tower which all on a sudden took fire and burned them, the grated windows preventing their escape. Spalding, a contemporary chronicler, narrates it as follows. "About midnight that dolorous tower took fire in so sudden and furious a manner, and in a clap, that the noble Viscount, the laird of Rothiemay, English Will, Col. Ivat, and others, servants, were cruelly burned to death. They hurried to the window looking out into the close; piteously calling for help, but none was or could be rendered them".

Dr Brebner, Forgue, once lectured on the burning of Frendraught, and gave a verdict of not guilty for Lady Frendraught, who was blamed for having set fire to the place: among other reasons he said that Spalding then alive did not blame her, but perhaps he was afraid to do so knowing the power that then could be exercised by the upper class. The ballad (which may have been written long after,) however, puts all the blame on her. The Crichtons seem to have declined after this, and today they lie in nameless graves. When I was at Bridge of Forgue we would at times during our dinner hour go to the kirkyard and give old James Scott a hand at digging a grave. James was a handloom weaver and crofter in addition to his work at Church officer. He told us that once when making a grave he dug up flannel that had been wound round the corpse in folds. He drew the attention of the minister to it, who, after looking up some old records, told him that he had opened a grave belonging to the Crichtons of Frendraught, and that the deceased's position in life accounted for the folds of flannel — the higher the position in life the more folds. Bones were removed from a grave in Forgue to one in another graveyard; someone asked James, who was digging up the bones, what he was doing this morning, James replies, "It's gettin' near the term an' folks man be flittin' ". At a term he changed his housekeeper and on being asked what sort of a woman the new one was, James said, "She's a kindly sort of a creature, but she'll stand no conter". A remark applicable to more ladies I doubt not. I neglected to say that in addition to his other duties, James was a butcher. Once he went to the manse to kill Mr Abel's mairt; preparations for this were going on in the kitchen when the minister found fault with James for not bringing someone to assist him. This he resented, telling him that he had killed over 200 good beasts, while this one was but a scratch of a creature he could take below his oxter, and in this indignant mood he went away without killing the mairt. In relating this incident James said, "There wis some women some lassies, an' auld Eppie Morrieson scrappin', an' cleanin' at onions, however, I bade them a good mornin' an' left". I did not hear when the mairt was killed. A day came when he passed away. I have mentioned him as being the last handloom weaver in Forgue, and other trades have vanished, and others are on the down grade. In former years many could earn or eke out a living at the slate quarries on Culsalmond and Foudland hills, but now no longer worked. Work could also be got at peat casting in the mosses, which are now all done.

Then divots were needed for roofs, but few I fear would now manage to work a flauchter spade. Then stot-thatchers found work, also dry-stone dykers; now little of either of this kind of work is needed today, although men to do either or both could still be found.

I have heard of a baker Nell about the Kirkton, at Auchterless, and presume that there had been a baking establishment there. There was one in Forgue for many years. There was a saddler too in both parishes. Now bakers and saddlers have all disappeared. And what about shoemakers and tailors? They have been greatly on the wane in past years. I do not think there is one tailor in Forgue while I am writing this in December 1923: in Auchterless tailoring is still carried on at 3 different places, but conjointly with other businesses or farming. Almost the same might be said of shoemaking, only it is carried on at 3 different places in each of the parishes, but more as shoemending than shoemaking concerns, making of new boots or shoes being now rare in rural districts. The decline in these 2 trades might be assigned to various causes, chiefly perhaps to the large amount of ready made clothing and foot-gear now worn, as likewise the introduction of the Parcel Post, which enabled the purchaser to buy direct from the manufacturer, thus saving the middleman's profit. I might mention other causes for the decline, as also other callings that are now waning.

FUNERALS AND FUNERAL INCIDENTS

Great changes have come about as regards funerals. In days of yore the dead were nearly all carried to their graves if the distance did not exceed six miles or thereby, unless the deceased or their friends had been above ordinary circumstances in life, when a hearse was employed. I remember when a hearse was kept at Roundhome, Forgue. The people turned out well to funerals in those days: and I have seen pretty trying carrying when the roads were blocked with snow and we had to find a way through fields. When the people assembled at the house where the dead was, they were served with a glass of port or sherry wine and shortbread but in the course of time that custom was given up thus effecting a saving to the poor.

When one died two neighbours went round the district inviting funeral folks, who almost without exception would

attend. The invitations usually were verbal, but letters were
delivered by the neighbours: having no beasts to look after I
came in for a fair share of this work. One was supposed not
to enter a house when he was performing this duty, some ill-
luck being attached to it. I did not always carry out this re-
striction however important it may have been.

.   .   .   .

The inviting by neighbours gave place to its being done
through the post, and now it is nearly all done by the newspapers. In the bread and wine days I was at a funeral where 3
or 4 of the dead man's near relatives, who came from a district many miles away, were present. We were in a school, the
bread and wine had been handed round, when the relatives
entered each with a glass of wine in his hand. One of them,
acting as spokesman, thanked the audience for their presence,
then partook of the wine. This was the only occasion I saw
this done, but it may have been customary where they resided.
An old man died suddenly at Glenythan, the fiscal caused a
post morten examination to be made. This was done after the
funeral folks had gathered to carry him to Auchterless,
[though] there was a snowstorm and the roads were blocked.
We had to wait a good while till the doctor had made the
examination, ere we got away; some of those who were to
attend the funeral on the Balgaveny side did not come to the
house, but were to join in afterwards. Not knowing the cause
for delay, they supposed that the funeral had gone by Logie-
Newton for a better road and, after waiting a reasonable
time, they divested themselves of their funeral attire; and so
when the funeral did come as expected they were unprepared
to give help which was much needed, it being necessary in
some places to leave the road and go through the fields. A
timekeeper walked in the front telling those carrying when to
change, so that all had an equal share in the work. One felt
their arms sore next day, but then there was the comfort that
a last and sacred duty had been performed. Apoplexy was the
cause of death.

.   .   .   .

When I was a young man I was at a funeral from North
Balgaveny to Drumblade. When we arrived there we found
about a foot of water in the grave, while the mouth of it was

all covered with mud, and while this did not trouble the dead, it was far from pleasant for the living; so into "a watery grave", the old woman was lowered. A tailor with whom I worked had disposed of his surplus clothing and through this I became the owner of a tile-hat, which I wore on this occasion, but as I thought that some of the funeral folks were taking special notice of me I never again appeared with it in public, and, by and by it disappeared.

. . . .

In 1893 I was at a funeral from Braeside of Rothmaise going to Auchterless. Distance necessitated the use of a hearse. When near Overhill, it came into my mind like a flash, the possibility of having horseless carriages propelled otherwise than by steam, in which electricity or chemicals, and perhaps both would play an important part. I lacked brains and means to carry out this daydream, yet I have lived to see it become a reality, through others; and now motor hearses and motors are at most funerals. Even the old custom of waiting at the grave till the last sod has been adjusted is abolished. The coffin is little more than covered with earth when a lid is put on the grave as a silent intimation to people to go away and leave the beadle to finish the work at his leisure. Mr Masson, Culsalmond, who officiated at this funeral from Rothmaise died in Aberdeen on 20th December 1923, aged 87 years, and was buried at Culsalmond, where he was 47 years minister previous to 1911, when he retired.

Many changes as regards marriages have taken place, as well as funerals. Changes on all hands.

NEWSPAPER INCIDENTS, ETC.

I remember well when the PEOPLE'S JOURNAL was in its infancy, and had but 4 pages. The stories in it were very interesting to me in those days; among others, "The Life of Mansie Waugh. Tammas Bodkin. Lucy, the Factory Girl" and others by the same writer — David Pae; among the last of them being, "The Lost Heir of Glencorran". Then there was "Mary Patterson; or The Fatal Error", a story of the Burke and Hare murders in Edinburgh; one of their victims being a well-known character — "Daft Jamie". Those were stirring times, many of the newly buried dead being taken from their graves and sold to the doctors for dissecting purposes, and many a strange tale was told about happenings in kirkyards, which were watched for a time after funerals. My father was among the watchers one night at Drumblade, but no resurrectionists appeared. Bodies were said to have been removed from Culsalmond, and the following story relates to that district. A body had been removed from a grave by two men and placed between them in a vehicle in an upright position. All went well till they halted at an inn on the north side of Bennachie, where they were to partake of refreshments. Two dismounted [and] went into the inn, leaving the man in the middle, who was said to be of temperate habits, in charge of the pony and trap. While the two men were at their refreshments an hostler removed the dead man and took his place. In a short time the two resumed their seats and the journey, but had not gone far when one of them remarked that their companion was warm. The man in the middle made answer saying, "If ye'd been for I wis ye'd been warm tee". The two fled, more perhaps for "safety" than for "succour", and the hostler was left in possession of pony and trap. I expect the dead man was again put back to his grave.

I can recollect the first time I saw the PEOPLE'S JOURNAL. My father had bought a copy, and seating himself at the fireside said, "Come awa' an' sit doon an' I'll read a story to you". It was to be continued the next week, and so was the paper. I read some of those stories in after years, but somehow they had lost the charm they had for me in life's gay morn. Another paper that came into our house was I think the Aberdeen Herald. It had several readers, my father being the last one, when it was nearly a week old. It had a racy article dealing with current events, written by Samuel Martin, the hatter, and usually ending with "so thinks Martin the hatter". I had to go past Mr Milne's, Upper Lenshie, once a week for it was on my way home from school; I liked this job, as I always got a piece from the housekeeper, Jane Gordon, but there was one terrible draw back for me. Mr Milne had a sister who was weak in intellect, and who lived in a house at the farm. She was very fond of young folks and wanted to get in touch with me, but I was much afraid of her: she had but to appear in order to make me quickly disappear. Mr Milne had a daughter named Hellen with whom I was at school, we also in after years both worked together at harvest work on her father's farm, then in the hands of her cousin, Mr James Lumsden, who succeeded his uncle when he died but is now at Downies, Inverkeithnie. He was a most agreeable master to be with. The following is from an Aberdeen paper, 1923. "SMITH. — At 26 Holburn Road, Aberdeen, on the 7th December, Hellen Milne, widow of James R. Smith, late of Hassiewells, Auchterless, in her 76th year. Funeral on Tuesday, the 11th instant, at 2 o'clock, to Springbank Cemetery. All friends cordially invited. This the only intimation and invitation".

And so another association with school days and maturer years, passes away. How true the words! — "Lowly we bend schoolmate and friend, passing away to the tomb".

Sometimes I sent advertisements to the People's Journal and these all duly appeared. An old woman died in the district, and her relatives put the matter on my shoulders, of seeing that some notice be taken of her in the PEOPLE'S JOURNAL. This I promised to do, proposing to go to Alexander J.M. Troup, at Bissitmoss and get him to do it, but a storm came on and had I written to him it would have been too late for that week, so I wrote a few lines and sent them on direct to the Journal office: but alas it never appeared, and she passed away unhonoured in the P.J.

Soon after this, changes were to be effected in the district that were known to me earlier than to reporters further afield, so I sent particulars to a daily newspaper and this was made use of, and reproduced in the P. J.; I consoled myself over the non appearance of the tribute to the old lady's memory, as unknown to them they were indirectly indebted to me for "copy". I had got upsides down with them. By and by I became correspondent for the P.J. in Balgaveny district from February 1906 to September 1912, when I left the district, receiving commission for all I sent, news excepted. I reproduce a tribute I paid to William Duncan, Middle Hassiewells who died on the 17th April, 1908. His brother George died at Balgaveny, in February 1917, after a short illness.

.   .   .   .

Another short notice that appeared in the People's Journal, was when my cousin, Mr William Mitchel, died at Balgaveny on 24th November 1909. — "There has just passed away a well-known and highly respected residenter in the person of William Mitchell, crofter, Balgaveny, at the ripe age of

85 years. He was born in the Alford district, where he was engaged herding cattle at an early age. About that period his father entered on the croft at Balgaveny, and on his death he was succeeded by William. When the "gatherings" were held at Badenscoth more than half a century ago William was known as a good runner, and he gained some prizes. He was a member of the Ythanwells Established Church, was a Conservative in politics, but took no part in public affairs. He is survived by a widow and grown-up family".

His eldest son John died 24th August 1915 aged 59 years: and his widow on the 14th May, 1921 aged 90 years.

"Thus star by star declines, Till all have passed away".

"JOY AND SORROW INTERMINGLED"

On the 5th December 1896 I was married at the Old School, Gariochsford by Mr Wishart, United Free Church of Forgue, to Jane Morrison, granddaughter of the late John and Mrs Morrison who are mentioned on page 70. This led me to experience what one Aaron Smith set forth in verse. Among other things he says, —

"How sweet when busy day is o'er,
And calculating cares retreat,
To pass my lowly cottage door,
And find a home made clean and neat;
Their heaps of wealth let others pile,
O'er their domains spread far and wide:
I'll ask contentment and the smile
That consecrates my own fireside".

On the 31st of December 1898 we laid our firstborn — Jeannie, in the grave at Ythanwells, she having died from diptheria aged 14 months. I insert the following by Mrs Sigourney, on the

DEATH OF AN INFANT

"Death found strange beauty on that cherub brow, And dashed it out. There was a tint of rose on cheek and lip; He touched the veins with ice and the rose faded. Forth from those blue eyes there spoke a whispered tenderness — a doubt whether to grieve or sleep, which Innocence alone can wear. With ruthless haste He bound the silken fringes of their curtained lids for ever. There had been a murmuring sound, With which the babe would claim its mother's ear, Charming her e'en to tears. The spoiler set His seal of silence. But there beamed a smile, so fixed and holy, from that marble brow, — Death gazed, and left it there; He dared not steal the signet-ring of Heaven".

"She set, as sets the morning star, that goes not down behind the darkened west, nor hides obscured amid the tempests of the sky, But melts away into the light of Heaven". — R. Pollok.

On 6th May 1900, the vacant place was almost filled, but that "almost" caused blighted hopes. On 4th April 1902, a son made his appearance, and came to stay. He has reached manhood and is a postman, and still under the parental roof. Early in 1910 my wife's health failed. After trembling in the balance for months, the end came on 20th June in that year, and as I was handy at house-keeping I acted on the advice of friends and became housekeeper myself; benefiting by the experience of former years at Forgue.

I quote the following by an anonymous writer in "The Christian's Penny Magazine" for 1865 on The Loss of a Wife, it says — "In comparison with the loss of a wife, all other bereavements are trifling. The wife! she who fills so large a space in the domestic heaven; she who busied herself so unweariedly for the precious ones around her, bitter, bitter is the tear that falls upon her cold clay! You stand beside her coffin and think of the past. It seems an amber-coloured pathway, where the sun shone upon beautiful flowers, or the stars hung glittering overhead.

.   .   .   .

There is so strange a hush in every room no light footsteps passing around, no smile to meet you at nightfall. And the old clock ticks and strikes and ticks — it was such music when she could hear it! Now it seems a knell on the hours through which you watched the shadows of death gathering upon her sweet face. And every day the clock repeats that old story. Many another tale it telleth too — of beautiful words and deeds that are registered above. You feel — oh, how often — that the grave cannot keep her".

The above will I doubt not appeal to many who have experienced this great loss. At this trying time as on other occasions I had many tangible evidences of the good feeling those among whom I moved had towards me — a feeling that the passing years has not extinguished. On my retiring from postal work in 1921, having reached the age limit, I was made the recipient of a wallet and treasury notes: of this I quote from the BANFFSHIRE JOURNAL of 6th September 1921; the only change I make on that report is that the old woman was named Mary and not Nellie. She had the letters in a basket with lids which was called a "riddicel basket" if I mistake not.

AUCHTERLESS

"PRESENTATION. — Mr Robert Barclay, senior on the completion of his term of service first as postman for 18 years in the upper district of the parish and latterly serving for a period of 9 years the district from Auchterless station by Blachree and Brownhill, was waited upon the other evening by a deputation at the farm of Upper Loop and made the recipient of a wallet containing upwards of £14, subscribed by friends in the latter district, which he has so faithfully served and in which he was so much esteemed. Mr George Smith, Greenbrae, in making the presentation, referred to Mr Barclay's unfailing regularity, his faithfulness, and most obliging qualities, and the regret all felt that he had to retire. Had it not been for the age limit, Mr Barclay seemed fit to undertake duty for a long time yet. However, they had to bow to the inevitable and wished him long life and health in the days yet to come. Mr Barclay, in reply thanked all the kind friends who had subscribed to the gift and remarked that he thought it needless to present him with anything as he had been so well rewarded from time to time in the course of his daily rounds. He felt sorry at having to give up duty, as it had been a real pleasure to him to have gone his rounds amongst so many kind people. He referred to some of the old customs of letter-delivery when he was a boy when old Mary went round with the letters, her fee being a bawbee on delivery, and such-like arrangements, which long since have given place to the more up-to-date methods. The company were hospitably entertained by Mr and Mrs Shirran, Loop".

Others of the deputation were, Mr John Gray, Brownhill, Mr and Mrs Gall, and Mr James Hendry, The Station; and Mr and Mrs Patterson, Woodend.

I received the following from the assistant postmaster Mr H.G. Neill, dated 27th July, 1921: "Mr Barclay senior auxiliary postman, Auchterless Station: Intimation has been received to proceed with your retirement, and the 30th of August 1921 has been fixed as the last day you require to attend for duty. I beg to express the appreciation of the Department of the way you have at all times performed your duties". (Signed) H.G. Neill, acting Postmaster.

On 5th September I had a note from Mr W. Russell, Postmaster at Turriff as follows, — "Dear Mr Barclay: On consulting the records here I find that you entered the Post Office service on the 25th of August, 1894; so that you have served the Post Office as an Auxiliary postman for the long period of 27 years. During the whole of that time you have given the utmost satisfaction to the Department, and the public and I greatly regret that the age limit necessitates your retiral. With best wishes W. Russell".

When I began posting, the late Mr Alexander was postmaster. He was succeeded by Mr Stuart, who retired upon his reaching the age limit. He was serving his apprenticeship with a merchant in Buckie, who kept the Post Office, when I was working with Mr Silverstine. When he came to Turriff I remembered having seen him in that shop. He was followed by Mr Russell.

I have omitted to mention the trouble — apart from the expense that Mr and Mrs Shirran put themselves to, at the presentation. But we all heartily partook of the good things provided for us, knowing the goodwill with which it was given.

One contribution to that night's programme I must mention, viz. Mr James Hendry's exhibition of ventriloquism in the dialogue on "The killing of a Pig", into which he introduced some items in keeping with the circumstances under which we had met. And so an eventful and, to me, a profitable evening, came to a close.

THE BATTLE OF LENDRUM

. . . .

[Account of the battle (11th century) taken from the *Old Statistical Account.*]

After reading the above I thought I would like to see the scene of those battles of long ago, but found that the sites of all except the scene of the third day's fight, known as the "Bloody Butts", were unknown to any in the district: Donald's Field has vanished. The Bloody Butts are below the road leading from Birkenhills eastward, and the Backmill burn opposite Lescragie. The camp may have been where the farm house and steading now are, which would account for the disappearance of the tumuli etc. The first fight may have taken place near Keithan where, until removed by a farmer a few years ago, there existed a mound or some such relict having the name Donald associated with it. Presumably the Brownhills were at one time known as Lendrun, and Keithan being about a mile to the east, it is more than likely that Donald would have gone out to this to meet the advancing foe. This would have been a wild and uncultivated district in those remote and troublous times; a good deal of it being moss which is now well nigh exhausted.

[POSTAL DELIVERIES]

When I commenced posting I kept count of all the postal packets collected and delivered by me, and this continued till the end. The collection on Gariochsford walk was bigger than Lendrum one [of my] last 9 years. This is easily accounted for; as packets collected in the former were delivered much earlier than if sent by Forgue where they lay till next morning; so I got a deal which was not connected with the walk. Then a part of the Lendrum walk was near the post office and was rarely handed to me. During the 18 years at Gariochsford I collected 87,220 packets and delivered 109,024, a total of 196, 244. On Lendrum walk during the 9 years the collection was 47,358, delivered 144,570; total 191,928. Thus a total of 388,172 packets of all kinds passed through my hands during those 27 years, a bit under half a million. I wonder how many have kept a similar record?

I now bring these reminiscences to a close. If I have given

offence to any by exposing the shortcomings of some I have
mentioned, I beg their pardon, and would in defence remind
them that I have not always concealed my own. I trust these
reminiscences of past and present times may prove interesting
to readers. I know they will to many of a past generation,
not a few of whom have gone far

> "South the line,
> Or o'er the wide Atlantic Sea".

Our next door neighbour had six daughters, all of whom
with one exception, were older than myself. Now all save one
are dead, and she, while I write in February 1924 is 81; the
youngest was the first to go. The old faces have vanished, and
new ones taken their place. —

> "Their names are graven on the stones,
> Their bones are in the clay".

While setting the type for these pages — a rather tedious piece
of work, I minded on a lesson in a school-book which gave
me some encouragement, entitled, "Perseverance — William
Davy", that told of one who wrote a book, and failing to get
anyone to undertake the printing of it etc. got the use of a
printing press and did it himself, even doing the binding of
the volumes; but I write from memory and may not be quite
correct after 60 years. But by setting "a stout heart to a stey
brae", he conquered. My stock of type being limited, I could
not set up more than a page at a time and not even that without using different sizes, as some letters now and again ran
short. My worst difficulty was when words were left out and
no room for their insertion could be found: this led to other
changes being made so as to preserve the sense. I easily de-
tected printer's mistakes in books and newspapers, but somehow my own escaped my notice, until I was taking out the
type — too late for correction. Punctuation was guess work,
not having studied that branch of learning. Sometimes I mis-
spelt words, thinking I was right, sometimes I misplaced
letters when I knew the correct spelling, and the errors crept
in and passed undetected and uncorrected. Yet in spite of
numerous drawbacks I am nearing the end, having made the
book nearly twice the size I at first intended. The printing
press was purchased from Messrs McGuire, 14, Victoria
Street, Elton, Bury, Lancashire, England.

THE BURIAL GROUND AT YTHANWELLS

This was ready for the reception of the dead in **January 1880**, and soon after began to be made use of. The first **to be** interred was George Troup, Bisset Moss, brother of **Alexander** J.M. Troup, journalist, Insch. The next was a girl **Anderson**, about 18, from Newton of Auchaber; and on 18th **December 1883** was interred Jane Taylor aged 18 years, who **died at** Goukswell, Culsalmond, on the 14th, after a short illness. **She** was a member of our household at Glenythan and **related** through marriage. She was laid in grave no. 1, G section, **and** in this grave was interred Mrs Crawford, my half sister's mother, who died at Gariochsford, January 1892. She lived with us after her husband died in 1871. He was buried at Marnoch and so would she, had it not been prevented by a snowstorm that had blocked the roads. In grave no. 2, Jane Barclay, my aunt, aged 97 was laid December 1884; and also our Jeannie on 31st December 1898, and a still-born girl on 7th May, 1900. In no. 3, a son of James Walker's Kirkton Auchterless (then at Gariochsford) aged 8 months lies. Grave no. 4, contains the remains of my late dear partner in life.

In grave no. 5, old Bell Harrigerrie is buried. She lived in the Drumdollo district; I knew her from boyhood. The name Harrigerrie now has become extinct; the Harri having been dropped, it changed into Gerrie. In the adjoining section lies an uncle's wife who died in December 1898, and 3 grandchildren. Her husband died many years previous to this and is buried at Auchterless.

Their oldest daughter, and youngest son are buried at Folla Rule, and the second daughter at Turriff. A parting time comes, and so does

THE END